MW00944764

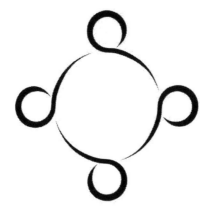

CIRCLE
OF WISDOM

A PATH FOR LIFE, MIND AND LEADERSHIP

ROBERT C. STONE

Circle of Wisdom –
A Path for Life, Mind and Leadership.
© 2015 Robert C. Stone

This story is designed to reflect accurate information in regard to the subject matter covered. It is sold with the understanding that through this book the author is not rendering psychological or other professional services. If expert assistance or counseling is needed, the services of a competent professional should be sought.

The Quadrenzo was designed by Robert C. Stone. Book cover artwork by The Islanders, Inc.

www.WisdomLeader.com

ISBN-13: 978-1511518475
ISBN-10: 1511518472

to Anna K.
without whom this path
would never have been possible

ACKNOWLEDGMENTS

It will be obvious *after* reading Circle of Wisdom that my debts of gratitude extend beyond any list of influential mentors, business partners, friends and family members. I owe it all to everyone.

And if I were to ever win an Academy Award, I would end my speech there, I promise. But here I will take the opportunity to mention some of the key people who have helped me make this book a reality. To the executive management of ATI Wah Chang for the courage to look within and giving me the opportunity to take their leaders through the first ever week-long training in these principles.

To my agent, Peter Miller of Global Lion Management. A major literary figure who took a chance on an unknown writer, and that just doesn't happen anymore. And for the professional editing of bestselling author Lou Aronica. I've edited other writer's books, stories and articles, but you can never consider your own work ready until a professional other than yourself has taken their turn with it.

To Marlene Balingit – we had so much fun on those national speaking tours (where I made all the promises to publish this book…)

To my core team in Nevada where we executed definitive proof of these concepts including superintendent Mark Stets who took a chance and believed we could make a change; to Randy Owen, who reads everything I write, not just with a critical and supportive eye, but with true enthusiasm and appreciation; and to Michael Karagiozis, my Chief of Medicine who became my best man and remains a source of brilliant dialog, spiritual balance and constant support.

To those who have provided spiritual support, teaching, or presence, including Krishna Das, a loving example of a human following love and sharing it. Who always takes the time to write me back the words I need to hear, whether they are the ones I want to hear or not. To Swami Ramananda who has provided me with the rare opportunity to see a man follow a devotion with every molecule of his being, and who shares unreservedly his wisdom and gifts with those who ask. And to all the priests, monks, ministers and others who prefer to remain nameless or who have already departed this life.

To my mother, Billie, and my late father, Robert J., who raised me with a belief in the power of story and taught me to speak in my own voice. They are with me in every word.

To my children, Katherine, Nicholas, Robert J (II), and Ceba T., from whom I have learned numerous lessons, both joyful and devastatingly painful. I bring from parenting the knowledge that there is no emotion that has the power to stop us from moving toward that which we truly value.

And to Anna, my wife and partner. It took me almost a lifetime to find you. It's still scary to think how close I came to never experiencing the love and life describable only by the poets.

There are many friends who have already come and gone in my life since I first wrote Circle of Wisdom that I will never forget. And to everyone mentioned here, and everyone not mentioned here, I express my gratitude which I hope remains undying even after I am not here to maintain it.

Thank you all.

INTRODUCTION

I grew up on stages and at Chamber of Commerce meetings. Somehow I developed passions for leadership and public speaking. I've also been an osteopathic physician for twenty years specializing in psychiatry. About ten years ago, I saw the intersection between the challenges of working in business team settings and my work, particularly with trauma survivor populations.

The latest cognitive therapies are based on modern neuroscience interpretations of ancient teachings designed to decrease suffering and seek the wisdom we all have inherently available within us. About this time I was invited to give my first week-long Fortune 500 training in Wisdom Leadership. It was an intense and life-changing experience.

A decision I made at that time was that the best way to transmit this knowledge, this process, was by telling it as a story. This book is that story. Stories give readers the opportunity to resonate and absorb as they are ready. They can discard and keep as they choose, then re-read at the right time.

Since giving that initial training, I have promised though various media to more than 4 million people that I would make this book available to the public. Now seems to be the right time to make good on those promises.

What I won't do here is talk about these principles. That's the story's job. I will let you know that this is not just a theoretical path, though. I have tested, honed and proved on my own and with many talented peers the effectiveness of the Circle of Wisdom in developing new business teams, healing broken corporate and agency systems and 'turning around' a large state healthcare program strangled for years by typical bureaucratic practices.

My first leadership role was as a manager for an AMC Theater in Dallas while I was still pre-med. During medical school, I co-founded Education Research Laboratories, Inc., which became an Apple award winning innovator and one of the first producers of handheld medical references.

I have had numerous leadership roles within medicine, culminating in a year as the Medical Director for the Southern Nevada Adult Mental Health System. A state auditor during my tenure there declared that, "In thirty years of auditing, I've never seen a state agency turn around in four months."

And the process continues, the path goes on. Now I think it's best to let the story do the rest. Read. Enjoy. Take what you think will work for you. And if you are so inclined, join in the conversation at WisdomLeader.com.

Peace,

Robert C. Stone
April 4, 2015

Robert C. Stone

CHAPTER 1

If they'd taken a moment to notice it, the three managers of Cooker Hills Ranch might have appreciated the bright sunshine that intensified the lush greenery around them. Such observations were not on the agenda today, though. The managers saw this day the way they saw most of the days on the ranch – as one filled with anxiety and aggravation.

"I don't know how anyone could expect us to deliver these production quotas," said Nay, the goat manager. Charged with maintaining a constant flow of goat milk for sale, he knew he had the most important and demanding job of anyone at Cooker Hills. "This place bleeds me dry and twists my insides into knots, and *still* what I do is never good enough."

"The way the boss cracks the whip around here, you'd think we were one of those huge corporate farms. It really riles me," said Ruf, the chief herd dog. His job – which he knew was the most important on the ranch – was to get the goats and chickens in the right places at the right times.

"Never, never, never," said Pek in the clipped tone he often used. Pek was the rooster manager of the hen house. He wasn't even sure why Ruf and Nay were on the same level on the organization chart as he was since egg production was the most vital function on the ranch. "We can never go corporate because the boss doesn't have the guts to handle that kind of pressure."

Nay tore some grass from the earth and looked back up at his colleagues while he chewed. He swallowed hard and said, "I give this place everything I have. I stay up late working on new production concepts. My wife hates the hours I put in. I worry about the ranch all the time. Do you know it took me 17 weeks just to develop the program that promised goat milk production would increase indefinitely? I can't even talk about it."

Ruf growled in agreement and walked a little closer to Nay. "I know what you mean about your wife. Mine *hates* how much I think about the ranch and how it affects my mood at night. I can't help it, though. It's frustrating to think about how many different management ideas we try around here – especially since most of them don't work.

Remember how the boss wanted us to wander around and talk to everyone more? Everything was supposed to be magically better once we did. I walked every acre of this farm 'til I thought my feet were going to fall off. How'd that work out?"

"Not the worst – no sir," Pek said. "Worst was that empowerment thing. Empower the lower animals – great idea. How do you keep 'em under control if you give 'em more power? Won't happen again, I promise you!"

Pek stabbed at the dirt a few more times and then sat down, seething. He got together with Nay and Ruf every day to blow off some steam but today's session was even hotter than usual because the ranch owner, old man "OM" Cooker, would return tomorrow from a three-month trip where someone was supposedly training him in something called "Wisdom Leadership."

The group remained silent for a bit, all three with their heads to the ground in various ways. Finally, Nay spoke up. "What do you think this 'Wisdom Leadership' thing is all about?"

"Same ol' same ol'," Pek said sharply.

"Old garbage in a new bag," Ruf grumbled.

"So we treat it the way we treated the other initiatives?"

"Of course we do," Ruf barked decisively. "OM may be the boss, but he doesn't have a clue how to do our jobs. Just pretend to take it seriously and then watch it fail like all of the others."

"Bosses, bosses, bosses," Pek said.

"Wisdom leadership," Nay spat. "OM will never learn."

Ruf stuck a paw in the goat's direction. "You got that right!"

As was so often the case, the stress level was higher now than it was when Pek, Nay, and Ruf started this conversation. In fact, each of the managers felt so stressed that they were speechless. The three stood stonily, staring off in the distance. Tomorrow did not seem promising.

* * *

The next day brought a flurry of activity. Word reached the managers by their morning meeting that OM Cooker was back – and that he had brought someone or something with him. Ruf, Nay, and Pek raced to the main house where they saw the owner's truck in the driveway. Attached behind it was a large trailer.

"Horses!" Pek said. "He brought back horses, horses, horses."

"Oh, no, not horses," Nay said, shaking his goateed chin.

"Pek! Nay! Ruf!"

The call came from the porch of the main house. It was OM, and though his voice cut the air with authority, there was something light in it, as though he was genuinely happy to see his managers after a long time away.

The goat, dog, and rooster ran toward the tall man in overalls with white beard and glasses. OM was the third in a line of ranchers who had owned and worked the goats and chickens of Cooker Hills Ranch. They climbed the steps and took their usual places in front of the rancher.

"Welcome back, OM," the three said in unison.

"It's good to be back," OM said grinning broadly. "How have things been since I left?"

"Fine, fine, fine," Pek said.

"Just great," Nay added.

Ruf barked proudly. "Really, OM, things couldn't be better,"

They nodded their heads, turning toward each other in agreement.

OM burst out laughing, something he'd never done in front of his managers before. In fact, everything about him seemed a little different.

Pek's eyes narrowed as he watched his boss. He thought about the horse trailer and wondered what it could mean to his standing on the ranch. If he'd only gotten those hens to increase output ten percent like he'd promised. His hens just sat around and squawked with each other. He could never get them dedicated to the new production quotas.

Nay was very worried. He had always lived in fear that OM would find horses more lucrative for the ranch than goat milk. Now OM had returned from whatever that wisdom thing was and he'd brought horses, Nay's worst nightmare. Nay wondered if OM would still need at least a few goats – to mow the weeds and that sort of thing. He resigned himself to the idea of running a mowing crew. At least that was better than the alternative. The alternative was unthinkable.

Ruf tried to think positively. Horses would definitely require dogs. The ranch might need fewer of them, but he was manager. His job was surely safe, wasn't it?

OM stopped laughing, though he still had a glint in his eye. "Oh, you guys. I've trained you so well, haven't I?"

"Yes sir, you have," Pek said.

"We're the best team you've ever had," Nay added.

Ruf agreed. "Couldn't be better."

OM offered another chuckle. "No, that's not what I mean. I mean that I've trained you to lie straight to my face."

The three managers fumbled over themselves. In a flurry of fur, feathers, and more fur, they assured OM that wasn't the case. Pek offered to present data at the morning meeting tomorrow and Nay said they had an outside auditing report to show that things really couldn't be better.

OM burst out laughing again. "This is truly amazing. As much control as I tried to exert over you, I never knew *how much* control I really had." He took a deep breath and a stillness came over him.

He looked down at his charges with a bit of his old gravity. "Noon," he said, the laughter gone from his voice. "Meet me at the trailer."

CHAPTER 2

At noon, Pek stood with the other two managers around the back of the big trailer. He tried to look his managerial best – folder filled with spreadsheets under his wing, beak tipped regally upward – but inside he was uneasy. OM had put them through many changes in the past, but Pek never thought things would get so bad that the ranch would turn to horses.

OM stepped to the back of the trailer, unhitched the doors, and swung them wide open.

Whatever was in the trailer was furry from behind. *Definitely* not a horse. That was good news, right? Pek felt a surge of bravado enter his bloodstream with the realization that they weren't going to be dealing with horses.

OM backed the animal down the ramp onto the ground.

A llama?

What was Cooker thinking? Was he thinking at all?

Pek leaned toward the others. "Llama fur? Cashmere? It'll go over like a lead balloon."

Ruf hacked like he was choking on a shard of bone and then whispered slowly and distinctly, "Consultant."

Pek nearly laughed aloud. Of course OM wasn't planning to raise llamas on the ranch. The llama was some kind of consultant. The relief almost made him giddy. No matter what the consultant was going to try, the managers could simply wait him out. They'd handled consultants before. This was old news. It was amazing, actually, that OM still threw his money away on them.

OM turned to them, an expression that bordered on giddy on his face. "Gentlemen, I'd like to introduce you to Dal."

The llama bowed low to them and slowly raised his head back, making eye contact with each of the managers in turn. Pek stared at him coldly, wanting to send the message that he knew what this furry animal was all about.

"Namasté," said Dal.

"Namasté," repeated OM in a voice that Pek couldn't recognize. It actually gave the rooster a little chill to hear such an odd word come from the boss' mouth in such a strange way. Pek felt his tensions rising again.

Of course, Pek didn't have a clue what the word meant. It was obvious that Ruf and Nay didn't either.

Maybe the llama was a mind reader – something else to worry about – because he turned to the three of them and said, "Namasté just means that the spirit in me acknowledges the spirit in you. Namasté."

Ruf repeated the word, or at least a rough approximation of it, back to the llama. Nay did the same, though his rendition seemed even more butchered than Ruf's. Pek didn't like where this was going. He wasn't about to start speaking this wooly consultant's language on demand. He bent low and mumbled, "I'm nasty," making it sound a little like "Namasté."

The llama bowed to him and said, "If you say so."

Pek's feathers ruffled and he looked at the llama nervously.

"Okay, gentlemen," OM said in a voice much closer to his usual, "let's have a little chat." They followed OM back to the main house and sat on the porch. OM took his favorite rocking chair and nodded toward Pek.

"Pek, let's start with the hens. How's production?"

"Good, good, good," Pek said, slipping into the cadence he naturally used when the head of the ranch wasn't around. He caught himself and raised his beak upward to OM. "As I told you, OM – and I've got the folder here with the numbers – our projections are in line with modified evaluations of the historical numbers when we take into account the un-factored variables. I could run the numbers again, but I'm sure they'll come up the same."

OM smiled a half smile. "Pek, you have a new job here, as of right now."

The folder fell from under Pek's wing. Pages of spreadsheet printouts scattered across the porch.

"As of today, you are in charge of running the hen house. Every aspect of egg production and hen development."

Pek wondered if OM had been smoking something on his retreat. "But that's already my job."

"No, your job was to run around trying to manage the hens the way I wanted them to be managed. Your biggest job was to take the heat when production fell off. Your new job is different. It's *your* domain now."

"Great, boss. Sure thing. I'm your rooster for the job." Pek didn't believe a word. This sounded like more consultant-speak. They'd done some serious brainwashing on the old man this time.

OM turned to the llama. "This isn't going to happen overnight, is it?"

The llama simply tipped his head toward OM.

OM looked at the others. "Same thing goes for you, Nay, and you, Ruf. New jobs as of now. Nay, I believe you have the knowledge and experience to run the goat crews yourself. Ruf, I think you have it in you to be a great dog leader."

Pek could see that the others were as dubious of this "new direction" as he was. Still, OM sounded more committed to what he was saying than he'd sounded about this stuff in the past. If nothing else, this would be interesting while it lasted.

"So, if I'm running the goats, what's with the llama?" Nay said, motioning in the consultant's direction.

OM glanced at the llama with adoration. It made Pek's gut bubble. "I've spent the last three months with Dal. I've learned a lot and I've changed a lot. I don't expect you to believe me, but I'm inviting you to join me in making changes

16

that are very necessary. Necessary not just for the ranch, but for us as individuals."

Ruf made that hacking sound again. "OM, this sounds a little soupy. A little touchy-feely. Maybe if I was running Pugs or Shih-Tzu's this would go over, but I'm running working dogs. The real things. Touchy-feely will get me laughed off the hill."

OM held up his hands. "I'm not asking you to accept anything or do anything. I'm just asking you to keep an open mind. See if Dal has anything that might benefit you. Are you at least willing to listen?"

Pek saw Ruf struggle with the answer, but he said, "Of course" with his tail drooping.

OM turned to Nay, who nodded, and then he looked at Pek. "What about you, Pek? Are you willing to give this a shot?"

Pek's brain said "no no no." but he tipped his beak downward a bit and said, "Sure, boss." hating himself immediately for it.

"So," OM continued, "what I'd like you to do is to think about what changes need to take place in your departments. Dal is going to show you the way to go about making these changes."

The llama smiled at OM. "OM, I think you missed a few steps there somewhere."

OM shrugged. "I think this might be a good place for you to take over."

The llama looked them all in the eyes again and then began. "Since the very first time we as individuals became aware of our world, we have wondered how we fit in it. What our place in the world is. While we may never have the final answer to this question, we often believe that our jobs have something to do with our purpose for living.

"If you look back over your lives so far, you will see that you've undergone numerous changes to make it where you are now. Pek, if you were the same rooster now that you were as a chick, would you be able to be the leader that you are today? Ruf, do you remember how excited you were when you were finally strong enough to run all the way up that hill? What it was like to look down on the valley from the top for the first time? Nay, I'm sure you have similar memories."

Nay nodded and Pek thought the goat was actually getting caught up in what the llama said.

"At some point, change, or the idea of growing, of things becoming different was exciting and important to you all. Why has it become so scary now?"

Nay spoke up. "I wouldn't say change is scary. It's been a long time since anything scared me. The point is that we don't need change any-more. How are we supposed to manage things when they are always changing? I've got the goats working right now and don't particularly want to come to work tomorrow and find that they are different."

"First," the llama said, "managing things is much different than leading a team. Trying to manage a bunch of changing *things* could be, well, difficult - if not scary. Leading a *team* is all about change, though."

"So there's no way around it?" Ruf asked.

"The way around it is the way through it. And that's what we're here to experience. Change used to be a dynamic, natural part of our lives, but somehow we decided we'd had enough change. Yet, we still suffer from things not being the way we want them to be. I'd like all three of you to think carefully about this question. In your areas of the ranch, on your teams, is there any-thing that needs to be different from the way it is now? Is something causing you pain or isn't as good as it could be? Anything at all?"

The llama let the group think in silence for a while. *You bet there are things that are causing me pain*, Pek wanted to say, but before the words could come out, Nay was speaking.

"I'm telling you Dal, I run a tight ship. And if you're here to tell me that I'm not good at what I do, then I'd vote that we save the money and send you back to whatever mountain you fell off of. You heard OM. He just put me completely in charge."

Pek had to give the llama credit. He took the shot from Nay and didn't bat an eye. Instead, he just looked at Nay intently. "Before you had your horns, Nay, could you butt heads with goats who did have horns? Did you consider yourself no good because you didn't have horns? Or was it that it just wasn't time for your horns yet? This is no different. Now is the time for a different kind of development. This doesn't have anything to do with being good or bad at your job or being a good or bad goat. It's just about your development and your ability to be the very best you can."

"Really, guys," OM said, "don't take the need for change personally."

The llama nodded. "Don't take it personally because it's not personal. Nothing is."

Pek thought this sounded like hogwash, still dumbfounded over how OM seemed to be buying into it.

The *consultant* continued. "The question to each of us now is whether there is anything that needs to change. Let's meet again tomorrow morning and you can tell me what you think. Thank you."

The llama bowed to them and walked down the steps and out into the pasture.

Pek felt like the sky had turned green. He looked over at Ruf and Nay and saw that they were as confused by the furry animal's words as he was. Then he looked at OM. OM's bright-eyed smile indicated he was not only taking all this seriously, but he was also enjoying it.

Slowly, Pek left the porch with the other managers. Something told him it wasn't going to be as easy to resist this change as the others had been.

And he didn't like that at all.

CHAPTER 3

Pek walked into the hen house still tense from the meeting with OM and the llama. He didn't have a clear fix on the llama yet, but if OM wanted to give him full responsibility, he was definitely going to take it. Forget this garbage about "Wisdom Leadership"; he'd show OM what *real* leadership was all about.

There were two hundred cackling hens in the house and not one of them shut up when he – the boss – entered.

There it was. The thing that needed to be changed *immediately* in the hen house. The hens needed to respect him more. Especially now that OM had put him *exclusively* in charge. He'd get his respect, all right. He was tired of being taken too lightly.

"Hens! Hens! Hens!" Pek shouted. The noise subsided slowly, though the cackling continued in several circles. It irked Pek that the hens didn't snap to attention when he called to them, but at least at this point, he could be heard above the noise.

"Listen! listen! listen!" he said rapidly and with increasing fervor. He realized he needed to dial things back a little and he took a deep breath. Then he continued. "I need to know why egg production isn't meeting the numbers we agreed on. I know I was clear when I told you what the new goals are. I took a course on corporate communication. The slides were in color, and you all received a copy of the memo. So, what's the problem?"

Now he had silence in the hen house.

* * *

Nay met with the chiefs of his goat teams, the meeting with OM and Dal still playing in his mind. It was more than a little bit strange, but it also gave him the opportunity he'd been looking for. For years, Nay had always been willing to take a stab at implementing whatever new management scheme OM came up with, always following the plan to the letter even when he was sure it would fail. No one could ever accuse him of not being a company man. Now, though, OM had given him what he truly wanted – even if he had a weird look in his eyes when he did it. He'd told him that he was the goat in charge of everything goat-related. Nay could really run with something like this.

"There are going to be some changes around here," Nay said in a tone that he thought was "presidential." "OM has put me completely in charge of all goat matters throughout the ranch. I'm it. I'm the top. This is not a democracy. If you'd like, you can consider it a benevolent dictatorship."

Nay looked at his chiefs and saw the fear in their eyes. He could already tell he was managing better. "I won't be doing any field work anymore. And I'm going to want your top goat as my assistant. As a result, you'll be down two goats on the rosters. I want new plans for covering all the shifts by close of business today."

Nay watched his chiefs gaze at him slack-jawed. It was not an inspiring sight.

"Also, we'll need to meet more. In addition to the midday meeting, I want a close-of-business meeting daily. This includes weekends. That's all for now. You have a lot of work to do."

A few of the chiefs nodded and the rest simply turned and shuffled back onto the ranch. They were about as motivated as a rusted-out tractor. *That's it*, Nay thought. *That's what needs to be changed. These chiefs need to put their hearts into their work. They just don't have the necessary dedication.*

* * *

Ruf had his meeting with the dogs that afternoon after getting updates from Pek and Nay. Like the two other managers, he had his misgivings about implementing yet another of OM's "breakthrough" schemes. Still, this Dal guy seemed different from any of the previous consultants and if the bottom line was that Ruf was going to get more autonomy, there was a chance this could work out okay.

Ruf tried to have all the dogs at each meeting, not just the assistant managers, and he encouraged everyone to talk at each meeting. Therefore, when he howled to announce the start of the gathering, he looked out on a large crowd.

"Nay has informed me that, due to a change in managerial circumstances, the goat chiefs will be busy for an hour midmorning and the last hour of the workday each day. When we take into account the managers' meetings the first of each day and the ranch-wide association meetings on Wednesdays, we're going to need to implement a complete reworking of the herding schedules immediately. With the increased egg and cheese production targets, that's going to mean more work done in less time. But I know we're all up to it. Does anyone see any problems?"

"There's definitely a problem with that plan, Ruf," an assistant manager said. "Dog feeding schedules are set by agreement with ranch ownership. If this has an impact on feeding, you can expect a no-go from the dogs. Goats get to eat all day long. No matter where they are, they are standing in the middle of their food. It's not surprising they don't take us into consideration in making these changes."

"Good point," Ruf said. "Assuming I get feeding ironed out, any other problems?"

Ruf spent the rest of his meeting, which ran long, listening to all the problems and all the reasons why the new plan couldn't and wouldn't work. The litany gave him a headache.

At the end of the meeting, he knew exactly what needed to change in his group.

* * *

OM watched as one by one the managers gathered with him and Dal on the porch the next morning.

"Namasté," Dal said when Ruf, Pek, and Nay had all arrived. Each of the managers responded with an approximation of the word, though it was obvious to OM that they neither understood the meaning of it or why Dal greeted them that way. He tried to comfort himself by thinking back to the first days of the Wisdom Leadership course and how it had taken him a while to wrap his mind around everything as well.

Dal began. "We left with a question yesterday. Have you come up with any answers?"

All three managers began at the same time, trying to speak over each other. OM thought this was a good sign that they were putting some energy into the process.

Dal restored the order. "Pek, you start. What changes do you need to make?"

"I'll tell you this much: at first, I thought you were way off base. Changes in the hen house? They just weren't needed. But I had a meeting with the hens yesterday and the answer slapped me right in the beak. The hens need to have more respect for my leadership. Especially given my new position. They need to see *me* as the boss."

Pek's words were like fingernails on a blackboard to OM. He frowned at Dal and received a calming expression in return.

Dal turned to Nay. "And you?"

"I felt the same way Pek did after the meeting yesterday, but then I realized that my crew chiefs do need to change. They need to put their hearts into their work. I don't see the dedication that should be there. I've already implemented changes to help with this. New meetings, a new schedule, and I'm out of the field now so I can put all of my time into my new position."

OM had a feeling he knew where that was headed, but he held his tongue.

"Ruf?" Dal asked.

"You know, I've got goodhearted, hardworking dogs on my teams. But they always come up with reasons why things won't work. I do a good job of asking them if they see any problems, but they always come up with way too many. This new schedule Nay came up with has practically caused a revolt. You know what needs to change for the dogs? They need to quit coming up with problems. Quit coming up with reasons why my plans won't work. I'm tired of it!"

OM felt a pain behind his eyes and fought the urge to pinch the bridge of his nose. He needed to let Dal handle this, at least for now.

Dal handed each of the managers a card. On the card was printed:

I must take my journey first.

"Let's read this aloud," Dal said. At first, the only voices came from Dal and OM. Dal very calmly prompted the group to read the card *together*. The second time, they did so, but they didn't exactly shake the windows with the volume.

"If you've never said it out loud," Dal said, "you've never heard yourself say it. How can you tell if you believe it or not if you don't listen to yourself?"

Ruf held up the card. "You gave us a question to answer and we all answered it. What's with the bumper sticker?"

OM felt compelled to break in. "When I changed your jobs yesterday, I was changing your job description from managers to leaders. The first principle of leadership is this 'bumper sticker.' What 'I must take my journey first' means is that you can't lead anyone somewhere you haven't already been. I've been starting my journey the last three months."

Dal nodded toward OM and then addressed the others. "All three of you have decided what you want to change in your outside world, in your groups or teams or workers. The question for you today is this: because you wish your outer world to be better, can you see that the change needs to happen in your inner world first?"

"Hold it, hold it, hold it," Pek said. "How's this all of a sudden about me?"

Dal set benevolent eyes on Pek. "There is only one person you can change and, fortunately, only one person who needs to change."

"But my crew chiefs need to change," Nay said. "They need more dedication. They need to put their hearts into accomplishing their goals."

"And my hens need to respect me," Pek said.

"And the dogs need to quit focusing on the problems," Ruf said.

Dal let each manager vent and then continued calmly. "Nay, you say your chiefs need to put their hearts into accomplishing their goals. Do they see you put your heart into their goals?"

"I put my heart into *my* goals. They should put *their* hearts into *my* goals too, because my goals are for the good of the ranch."

"Could it be that you and your leaders have different goals? And if so, why?"

Before Nay could answer, though – and OM wasn't positive that he could – Dal turned to Ruf.

"Ruf. Can you look at yourself and see if there's anything you do that encourages your dogs to focus on problems? You say you don't want them to focus on problems, but what do you want them to focus on? There may not be much difference between what they do and what you do."

Again, Dal didn't wait for an answer. He turned immediately to Pek. "You say your hens need to learn to respect you. Do you respect your hens? And if so, how do they know it?"

"No, no, no. I don't want them to respect me. I want them to respect my position, my *leadership*. This is just about work."

OM couldn't let this pass. "Pek, what I have learned after a long life of doing business is that when we are dealing with others, it's never just about work. There's always a chicken behind each hen. There's always a goat behind each crew chief, and there's always a dog behind each herd dog."

Dal smiled at OM. "Given that you have all realized change is necessary, and knowing that change must begin with yourself, do you believe change is possible? Do you believe you can change? Let's meet again tomorrow morning and you can tell me what you think. Thank you."

Without waiting for a response of any kind, Dal bowed to them and walked down the steps and out into the pasture. OM looked at his managers and knew that their heads were spinning. He knew that each of them had something to say to him and he also knew that further conversation wasn't appropriate right now.

He got up and walked into the ranch house.

CHAPTER 4

Ruf had plenty of work to do the rest of the morning and didn't have much time to think about the latest meeting with OM and Dal. Still, he found the words "I must take my journey first" rattling through his mind. Was there something to this? Probably not. And even if there were, his dogs didn't need a leader on a journey. What they needed was to learn a way to make things happen without stressing over why it *couldn't* happen. Ruf wondered how much OM had paid Dal for the three-month course that had turned him from a rancher to a sage. Whatever it was, it was *way* too much.

And yet, the words on the card cropped up repeatedly.

I must take my journey first.

After lunch, Ruf met with Pek and Nay outside the hen house. Pek was full-out agitated, stabbing at the dirt with his beak.

"Llama goes, llama goes, llama goes," he said heatedly. "I can't believe the garbage he tried to feed me this morning. We have to talk to OM about this."

"I wanted to say something to him this morning, but he just walked away," Nay said.

Ruf pawed at the ground. "I think Dal has OM wrapped around his furry tail, if you want to know the truth. I don't know what good it would do, but I'd be willing to back you up if you're willing to do the talking."

"Let's go, let's go, let's go."

The three of them headed toward the main house, Ruf trailing behind the others, unsure of the point of this exercise. As they rounded the corner, they saw OM sitting in his chair with Dal on the porch next to him. Neither seemed to be moving at all.

"Darn it," Pek said.

"I told you he was too into this consultant," Nay said. "We'll never get him alone now."

At that point, OM's eyes opened. It was too late to turn back now. Ruf and the others walked onto the porch.

"Namasté," Dal said.

"Yeah, whatever," Pek said. "We've got to talk."

Ruf nudged Pek with his nose and whispered, "Lighten up a little. If you make them mad, it's just going to make things worse for us."

Ruf's admonition seemed to have no impact on the rooster. Pek turned toward OM, beak high in the air and said, "Tell me, tell me, tell me. What have I done to earn this? Haven't I given you the best year of my life? I don't even plan on retiring; you know that. I could leave right now and spend the rest of my days over at Vegetarian Farms being eye candy for the kids in the petting zoo."

OM gazed at Pek calmly. Ruf was sure that before his three-month "journey" OM would have eviscerated Pek for his attitude. "Pek, it's precisely because you have been so dedicated that I am offering this experience to you."

"Nonsense, nonsense, nonsense. Haven't I done things the way you wanted them done?"

"Yes. You have, Pek. But that's exactly the problem. Well, not the problem, but the opportunity we have here. You did things the way I thought they should be done. This ranch runs at probably thirty percent of its potential and at 100 percent of the misery possible. I finally got tired of both. I went to Dal to find out how to change you all, and learned something entirely different."

"I must take my journey first," Ruf said, not even realizing the words had come out of his mouth.

OM smiled at him. "That, and much more."

"Pek, tell us what is on your mind." Dal said.

"I will, I will, I will. I'm tired of changing the way I do things and I'm just not going to do it anymore. I've been to every manager training and seminar OM has ever crammed down our throats. I know how to handle hens. I know the tricks and the techniques for motivating them."

Dal absorbed this quietly for a moment. "Pek, no matter how ornate your box, no matter how big or comprehensive it is, I won't fit into it. Drop the box. Drop the tools you learned to deal with me. Open your heart to me and to yourself and what we need to happen will happen. What you need to say you will say and what I need to hear, I will hear."

Ruf found himself nodding as he heard this. Then suddenly he snapped out of it. There were practical issues to address here. "So you want us to have a tool-less toolboxes? I've got a bunch of purebreds to run. It takes all the tools I have just to keep them in line. I mean, I have to ask them the right questions so they will come up with the answers I want them to come up with. That way they'll think it was their idea in the first place."

"Using questions to force someone into a conclusion is just a more subtle way of manipulating them," Dal said. "As long as you see others as needing your manipulation, you will never become a wise or effective leader."

Ruf found himself nodding again.

Suddenly Pek slapped him across the snout with a strong right wing. "You're not buying this stuff, are you?" Pek pointed his wing directly at Dal's nose. "It's either you or me, Dal."

Dal smiled at him. "Pek, there's room for all of us on this porch and there's room for all of us on this ranch. We're only asking you to bring an open mind and to develop an open heart to yourself and to others."

But Pek wasn't buying any of this. As Ruf tried to understand at least some of what Dal was saying, Pek shouted, "You haven't heard the last of me, llama!" and stormed down the steps off the porch.

"Hen house! Now!" Pek yelled to Ruf and Nay. Nay headed down the porch and Ruf reluctantly followed. First, though, he looked back at Dal and received an expression he didn't know how to interpret.

* * *

Pek felt his insides burning as he stormed into the hen house. He knew that Ruf and Nay were behind him, but he'd barely given them a thought during his rampage from the ranch house. Pek ran into the middle of the hens and screamed for them to shut up, wings flapping and feathers flying. Within seconds, Pek had complete silence.

Wow, he thought, *they can show me respect*. Maybe this was the kind of change OM and Dal were talking about. Maybe he just hadn't been yelling loud enough.

No, that wasn't it. Dal was a fraud and OM was a fool for believing in a fraud.

Pek turned to the other two managers, his eyes blazing. "Listen, listen, listen. Nay, Ruf, we've worked together for a long time. I expect your support on this. You can't let them suck you in. They are accusing us of being the busted ones. Us! Can you believe it?"

"They said not to take it personally," Nay said softly.

"Not take it personally? It's about *me*!" Pek pointed one of his wings right under the goat's nose. "Have you lost it? Dal is saying we are the problem. He's saying *you* are the problem. You have to take that personally!"

Ruf shook his head back and forth briskly. "Pek, I don't think this wishy-washy stuff is going to go over with the dogs. I really don't. But I think if you fight Dal and OM on this, it's just going to get worse. Can't you play along, for feathers' sake?"

"Ruf's right," Nay added. "To tell you the truth, your reaction to this is starting to irritate me more than all that Llama fur. Let's let them think we're following along with them. Let's make some changes. I know what I'm going to do starting tomorrow. The sooner we get this over with, the better. Then OM will go back to being his usual ineffectual self and Dal will be out of our lives."

Pek's respect for the other two managers was dropping by the millisecond. He wasn't going to go along with their ridiculous approach to this situation. He knew what he had to do and he was going to do it whether Nay and Ruf supported him or not. If OM wanted leadership, he was going to get leadership!

Pek stabbed the ground three times and walked away from the others.

CHAPTER 5

The next morning, Nay caught up with Ruf as the two walked over to the ranch house. He wasn't looking forward to another meeting with OM and Dal, and now he didn't even want to see his old friend Pek. He'd learned a long time ago that going through the motions was the best way to approach any disagreeable situation and he knew that if the managers just played at making an effort with OM and the consultant's new plans, everything would be back to normal soon enough.

Why fight authority when you know they're making a mistake? The mistake will prove itself soon enough. Pek, though, couldn't seem to relax about it the way he'd done in the past. Something had really set him off this time.

"That was quite the psychodrama in the hen house yesterday, wasn't it?" Nay said as they walked.

"Pek certainly seems to like to mix it up at times, doesn't he?" Ruf said

"Have you seen him this morning?"

"No, not at all. I figured we'd run into him on the way here. I certainly hope he isn't planning to go no-show on us. If that happens, he'll have to contend with me, too."

Nay had seen Ruf in his aggressive mode. If Pek knew what was best for him, he wouldn't bring out the legendary fury in the dog leader.

They turned the corner and headed toward the porch. Nay nearly stumbled backward when he found Pek already there chatting pleasantly with OM and Dal.

"Namasté!" Pek called, as if he'd been replaced by his jovial twin.

"Namasté," Nay and Ruf replied, glancing at each other confusedly.

"Guys, I've decided that Dal and OM are right. We need to change and it has to start with me. I'm ready. I know you have doubts, but I hope you get over them. I'd hate for you to miss this opportunity."

Nay was speechless. When he'd last seen Pek, the rooster's eyes were bulging out of his head. Now he seemed relaxed and compliant. This couldn't be good, but Nay felt he had no choice but to play along.

Dal, who may have been accustomed to combatants turning into acolytes overnight, started the day as though everything was normal.

"The first principle of leadership," he said, "is 'I must take my journey first.' The first step in change is understanding that change is needed. The second is to believe that change is possible. That was your question from yesterday. Do you think change is possible?"

"Change is definitely possible," Pek said enthusiastically. "Definitely."

Nay stared at Pek, even though the rooster looked away. After a moment, Nay realized that Dal was expecting a response from him. Nay threw one more glance at Pek and then said, "Yes, I think it's possible, and I'm looking forward to implementing it today."

"Ruf?" Dal asked.

"Give me a second here." Ruf took two slow steps toward Pek. "I don't know what kind of soup you're stewing here," he growled, "but I don't feel like being an ingredient in it. Just yesterday you were running around like you had your own head cut off. What gives?"

Pek's eyes widened and Nay could see that he felt a little intimidated. If he were acting, though, he wasn't dropping the role. "Ruf, I just realized there's room for us all, and that change is important – no, mandatory. I thought a lot about this last night and I decided it was right to change. That's all that happened. Now, are *you* ready for change?"

"I thought I was, but now I don't know." Ruf turned toward Dal. "I don't feel like blindly following anyone."

Dal nodded as though he were expecting that exact response. "If we were supposed to follow anything blindly, we wouldn't have been given eyes. This isn't about a process that happens overnight. I encourage you to take your own journey. Help your friends where you can and accept their help when it is right to do so. But it's your journey."

"Given that," Ruf said. "I'd say change is both needed and possible, but I'm holding out for what's next. I keep waiting for you to throw me a substantial bone."

"Then let's see if we can get you something to chew on. This next part takes courage. What do you think requires the most courage in this world? What kinds of things require courage in your jobs?"

Ruf raised himself up immediately and said, "I fought in the Wolf Wars. Three times, I had to rescue young goats from the Grey Wolf League. That was back in '02. Before your time,

Pek. Is that the kind of thing you're talking about Dal?"

"Very good example, Ruf. It sounds like the Wolf Wars were very scary."

"I prefer to say that it took courage. I don't think anybody likes to talk about things being scary."

"You're right, Ruf. Very few people do. And yet, if the situation was not scary, it wouldn't have taken courage for you to protect the kids, would it?"

Ruf lifted a paw and patted it up and down on the porch. "It's getting a little squishy in here, Dal." He said that with a chuckle in his voice, though, and Nay could tell that some of this was having an impact on the dog.

Nay, of course, had his own memories of the Wolf Wars. "The Wolf Wars were tough. I was just a kid myself. I wanted to go fight, but they wouldn't let me. I did get to help with an evacuation, though."

"You were very brave that night, Nay," OM said. "It was storming too. Those were scary times."

The memory filled Nay simultaneously with a sense of pride and unease. He wanted desperately to go out into the fray during the wars to protect his home and his fellow goats. If anything

44

like that ever happened again, he'd be butting heads with abandon.

Pek clucked, which threw Nay back into the present.

"I can't say I was ever in a war," the rooster stated. "I guess my biggest act of courage was asking the missus to marry me. I was young, didn't have steady work yet. I knew she'd say yes, but you know, you never *really* know, until…"

Everyone nodded their heads in agreement, probably doing the same thing that Nay was doing – remembering how nervous he felt before he proposed marriage.

Dal said, "These are all very good examples of being brave and showing courage. Let's talk about what courage means. I know no one wants to discuss the idea of being scared or afraid, but it is a very important part of courage. Being courageous doesn't mean you don't experience fear. On the contrary. Having courage means facing a fearful situation head on. It's not whether you are afraid or not. Courage is the willingness to stand in the face of fear."

"So," Ruf asked, "now that we've all gotten in touch with this fear thing, what part of the change process requires so much courage?"

"It doesn't take much courage to point out what is wrong with someone else, does it? But to take a clear, honest look at ourselves and how we work with others takes *great* courage. Undoubtedly, we will see parts of ourselves that we don't want to see. But these things are exactly what we need to change in ourselves."

"This is going to take a little more explanation," Nay said.

"Of course. Let's look at a familiar situation. What are some circumstances where people have been really angry with you?"

"My chiefs have a tendency to get angry with me every time I implement a new plan, which makes me wonder even more about how these new changes are going to go over."

"Why do you think they get angry with you?"

"I don't know; maybe they just aren't good chiefs."

"Why else might they get angry when you change things on them?"

"Maybe they don't like having things changed on them any more than I do."

"Why wouldn't they like having things changed on them?"

Nay sighed. "Maybe they feel like I'm telling them they aren't doing a good job. I know that's kind of how I feel when OM starts in on all these change efforts."

Dal tilted his head sideways. "How do you feel when you believe OM doesn't think you are doing a good job?"

"Angry," Nay responded instantly.

"What else? What other feeling might be underneath the anger? Think again about your chiefs. What might they really be feeling when they are angry?"

"I guess they might feel inadequate or incapable, or at least they might think I feel that way about them."

"So, is it possible that you feel inadequate when OM springs a change on you?"

For something that wasn't supposed to be personal, this was getting awfully close to the bone. Nay scratched his goatee and checked his watch. "I'm going to have to think about that one, Dal – and it seems to me that we're running a little long this morning."

"This is as good a time as any to stop. I think we've made the point. If we are to look at ourselves openly, it is going to take courage. Our next step is to look at ourselves despite any fear we may have. Despite what we fear we will see. When we get angry, irritable, or act in a mean way, what are we really experiencing? What are we feeling underneath it all? Do we have the courage to look and see?

"Let's meet again tomorrow morning, and you can tell me what you think. Thank you."

Dal bowed to them and walked down the steps and out into the pasture.

CHAPTER 6

Pek laughed bitterly on his way back to the hen house. He loved the expression on Ruf and Nay's faces when he greeted them with that "Namasté" garbage. But what he loved even more was how gullible OM and Dal were. They really thought he'd bought into their plan. *Fools, fools, fools!*

When he looked back on things, he saw that OM had given him other opportunities to take charge in the past – but none were as wide open as this one. Pek was going to prove to OM that he had leadership tools way beyond anything some llama could teach. He was going to show that he had the skills to rule over much more than a stupid bunch of hens.

He entered the hen house and slammed the door. He walked into the middle of the room, spread his wings, and yelled, "Shut up!"

He turned in circles, looking at all the hens. His eyes blazed. The hens quieted some, but not nearly enough.

"I mean it. Shut up right now!" he screamed at the top of his beak.

What is up, he thought. *Yesterday I only had to yell once. How mad do I have to get to command their attention?*

"Maybe this will quiet you down." He waved a report for all to see. "My first act as supreme manager of the hens is going to be to fire ten percent of you. The worst ten percent. I'll let you figure out who goes and who doesn't. Hen coordinators – I expect your recommendations by close of business today."

Lucinda, one of the hen coordinators spoke up. "Pek, if we're trying to increase production by ten percent, how can we afford to *fire* ten percent?"

"The way I see it, the bad ten percent haven't been producing their fair share to begin with. Those who are left will know they'd better get their production in line or we'll make even deeper cuts. That's just the way of the world."

"Aren't there any other alternatives? Can you give us a week before you make a formal decision? This is the first we've heard about potential layoffs."

"I'm not talking about layoffs," Pek said sharply. "I'm talking about *firing*."

Lucinda took a few steps forward and dipped her beak. "But, Pek," she said in a hushed tone, "you know what it means for a hen to get fired."

Lucinda clearly misunderstood her place. Pek's ire rose. "Go, go, go! I've had way past enough from you."

Lucinda took a step back, but she held Pek's eyes. Lucinda was a valuable hen and a huge producer, but she'd better learn how things worked around here. Pek leaned toward her until his beak practically touched hers. "If you have any thoughts of going outside the hen house with any of this, you can consider yourself first on the firing line? Am I clear?"

"You'll get your recommendations, Pek," Lucinda said tersely.

"Then everything will be fine," Pek said, turning away.

* * *

"Can we just hold things still for a moment?" one goat chief asked. "We've been over and over this. We can't afford to lose our best worker to be your assistant since you're not going to be in the field yourself anymore."

Nay wasn't interested in any level of resistance from his underlings. "What? I've already given the new schedule to Ruf and the dogs. Management and ownership are already coordinating talks to renegotiate feeding schedules."

"It's just too much, too fast," the chief said. The other goat chiefs nodded their chins in agreement. "We've been through it every possible way. It doesn't seem like it's going to work."

The chief lowered his head when he said this and Nay thought the goat was actually planning to butt heads with him – something Nay was quite ready for at that moment. The chief seemed to understand what he'd done and quickly lifted his chin.

Nay relaxed and surprisingly found himself reflecting on Dal's words. As though someone else were speaking, he asked the chief, "How do you feel when I try to implement change?"

The other goat seemed completely confounded by the question. "What?"

"I think that when I try to implement change quickly like this, it makes you feel incapable and unworthy."

"What? No! I don't know what you're talking about. I'm just saying this plan won't work. It doesn't have anything to do with my feelings. Besides, I'm a crew chief. I know I do a good job."

Nay stroked his chin slowly. "I was once just like you. It takes courage to admit when you feel scared and vulnerable."

The chief's eyes showed fear, as though he were being ambushed. "Nay, is there something going on here I should know about?"

"I'm serious. If you don't figure out what scares you, you're never going to get anywhere."

"To tell you the truth, *this conversation* is starting to scare me."

"Good! Maybe that's what you need. Look, the bottom line is that the changes are happening. It's my call and I'm making it." Nay swept his eyes over all of his chiefs. "It's your job to implement it. Go do that."

* * *

Ruf couldn't stop thinking about the last conversation with Dal. That llama really had a way of getting under your fur. And as he started his meeting with the dogs, he couldn't help but wonder if this latest consultant might actually be making the tiniest bit of sense.

Ruf barked sharply to call the meeting to order. "We all know this new plan from the goat teams has caused no end of challenges, but I'm sure we are up to it. I'd like to hear your feedback."

An assistant manager spoke up. "Ruf, the feeding schedule is what's on most of our minds. What's the latest?"

"Ownership and management are meeting, as usual, on Wednesday. All the ranch schedules are on the agenda."

"We can't get a quicker answer than that? This is a huge issue."

Ruf snorted, wondering if he'd ever have a meeting that didn't start contentiously. "I assure you all that we will find a solution to the feeding schedules. No one is going to go hungry. Mealtimes might be changed, but we know to expect that now. Can we concentrate on our part?"

Another dog spoke up. "How do you expect to cover security for the hen house while we're out herding three goat crews, instead of just two like usual?"

"I've been thinking about that. We will team up on the crew that is nearest the hen house during each shift. That team will have to be on alert for security duty at the hen house, if necessary. Let's face it; security for the hen house is light duty. I mean, who doesn't spend most of that shift playing solitaire? Anybody see any problems with this?"

"Yeah, it won't work!" a dog yelled from the back of the group. The pack laughed.

"Very funny," Ruf growled. "Seriously now."

"I am being serious," the dog said, moving forward. "We have a very clear double duty clause in our contract and I believe it is there for a reason. Sure, hen house duty is a cinch, but if something happens, we can be out twenty to thirty hens just like that. It only takes one wolf."

"Yeah," another dog added, "and what happens when the closest goat crew isn't really close to the hen house?"

"What if the goat crew dogs are too far to signal security for backup?" another dog said.

Ruf felt like he was going to hack up his lunch. "Enough! Why do all of you always look at the worst possible outcome to every situation? I'm tired of spending all of our time talking about why things won't work. You were all hired because you could get the job done, but you seem more intent on *not* getting anything done."

He turned his back on the dogs and scratched dirt at them with his hind legs. He was sure the message of that gesture was lost on no one.

As he continued to walk away, one of his assistants caught up to him. "Can I talk to you without your biting my head off?"

Ruf bared his teeth, but then he turned to the dog and chuckled. "I'm not making any promises, but shoot."

"Do you really want to know why we always tell you the problems with every plan?"

"If you can tell me that, I'm all ears."

"Remember, you promised not to bite my head off."

"Actually, I didn't promise that," Ruf said ominously. The other dog stopped in his tracks and Ruf laughed jovially. "But I'm promising now."

What he heard next rocked him at his core.

CHAPTER 7

Ruf was still emotionally wobbly when the group met on the porch the next morning. The feeling was somewhere between how he felt after eating some bad meat and how he felt after his wife gave birth to their first litter of pups. To compound this sense of hazy unreality, a light rain and mist surrounded the main house, separating the group from the rest of the world.

Dal welcomed them. "You are now beginning the way of the warrior leader. As you continue to look openly at yourselves, you'll understand why we call this process warrior leadership. You're not at war with anyone, least of all yourselves, but you have to develop the fearlessness of the warrior to complete this cycle. What are your experiences since our last talk?"

Dal looked straight at Ruf when he asked the question, as though he could tell that Ruf had a lot on his mind. "What if I don't want to talk about it?" Ruf said sharply. "You said this wasn't personal. Well, if it isn't personal, then I shouldn't have to do anything I don't want to do."

"It sounds like you might have experienced something very real," Dal said. "Don't you think what you felt is worth investigating?"

OM leaned forward in his chair. "Hey Ruf, I get what you're talking about. But facing our emotions is a key part of this process. If we don't, then no matter what we do, we can only make superficial changes."

Dal nodded. "OM is entirely right. Have any of you tried to implement changes with your teams without previously discussing those changes with them?"

"Of course," Nay said. "But we went to a seminar on that. We learned how to tell people about change so they could understand the rationale behind what was happening."

Ruf remembered that seminar and he remembered how little it accomplished. He pawed the dirt and then looked back up at Dal. "If you're trying to tell us we have to get everyone to understand the change first, we've been there, done that, and come home with our tails between our legs."

"You two are making my point for me," Dal said. "If you just tell your workers what to do, they will resist it. If you tell them what to do and tell them why you are doing it, they will still resist. Why do you think that is?"

Ruf pawed at the dirt so hard that he sent a stone in Pek's direction. The rooster gave him a dirty look in response. "Can't you just spit it out instead of asking a million questions? Just tell us what we have to do."

Dal laughed, which annoyed Ruf further. "Ruf, you don't just make my point, you *are* my point. What would you have thought if I'd shown up that first day and simply told you what to do? Are you telling me that you three didn't already have a plan to resist whatever I tried to implement? You probably thought of me as a consultant. How many consultants have come and gone here on the ranch?"

OM whistled, drawing Ruf's attention away from Dal. "Plenty, I'll tell ya. I can't say I'm proud of that. We've run through just about everyone who was willing to come out here. I wish I had a nickel for every nickel I spent on them."

"I understand you," Dal said. He turned back to the group. "External change is just that. External. You can't expect external change to cause an inner transformation. But you *can* expect inner transformation to cause plenty of change."

If Dal intended this to soothe Ruf's anxiety, it wasn't working. If anything, he felt more irritated now than he did when he arrived. He paced across the porch. "Look, I've seen what I did wrong. If I don't do it anymore, what's the problem?"

"If you make any change without examining and acknowledging your vulnerable emotions, then you are still making superficial change. You are still running from the root of your pain and the true cause of your problem."

Ruf stopped his pacing and glared at Dal. "Who wouldn't want to run away from the pain? Frankly, it sounds awfully masochistic to *want* to feel pain."

The llama laughed again and Ruf had an even stronger desire to swipe a paw at him. "Yes, indeed, it would be stupid to seek pain. However, if you develop the warrior leader's ability to see openly into himself, you will find whatever emotion is underneath the anger or irritation or depression and you won't have to run away from your feelings or indulge in them either. When you do this, two things will happen. First, you can learn to respond differently to the feeling. If you tend to get angry when you feel threatened, you can learn to recognize feeling threatened and choose to act differently. Second, by not hiding the underlying emotion, you give it a chance to run its course and dissolve just as it formed. Without this, it may stay with you as long as you live."

"All right," Ruf said. "I think I get this point. Either get to the core or forget it. We dogs have a similar saying. We say, 'The marrow is where the marrow is.' It's a bone thing."

"As long as it's not a goat bone," Nay said. "If this is the answer, then why did my goat chiefs miss the point yesterday? I told them that I know they feel vulnerable when I try to change things on them. I told them I knew they were feeling incapable and incompetent, but they wouldn't admit it."

OM shook his head and chuckled lightly. Ruf was glad the boss was chuckling at someone other than him. "What is the first principle of Wisdom leadership?"

"I know: I must take my journey first. But I had. We already talked about it."

"'I must take my journey first' usually refers to being on the journey more than thirty minutes," OM said, chuckling again.

"But it is good that you realized you had feelings of being incapable and incompetent," Dal said. "It took great courage to admit that."

Pek finally spoke. "Please tell us, Dal. What is it we must do next? What must we do now that we have acknowledged our painful emotions, as I have?"

"What emotions are you talking about?" Ruf growled, still peeved over being the main topic of this morning's session.

"*My* emotions," Pek said. "I've felt them and I've dealt with them – even if I haven't decided to share them with you."

Dal said, "You are right that you don't have to say out loud what you've found inside yourself. But in this group, at least the first time through, it can be a very good idea. Again, only if you feel safe doing so."

Pek remained silent and Ruf glared at him.

"I've got two issues Dal," Ruf said. "One, you referred to this as the first time through, so I assume this is something we have to do more than once. Two, you keep bringing up this 'feeling safe' thing. Feeling safe, feeling vulnerable. Safe, vulnerable. Blah, blah. What's the fascination with feeling vulnerable?"

"When you feel threatened, Ruf, like the stormy night when you faced the wolves to save the kids, what is the only thing on your mind? What becomes your sole purpose?"

"Survival, of course. When you're threat-ened, all you want to do is survive. But we don't have wolves running around here all the time."

"No, we don't," OM said. "But it doesn't take a wolf for us to feel threatened. I've lived on this ranch my whole life and I realize now that we all go around feeling threatened and threatening others. It's been a way of life here."

"Ruf, you mentioned that you had an in-tense experience yesterday," Dal said. "When you look back on it today, do you think you felt threatened or vulnerable at any point?"

"I thought we didn't have to discuss this stuff out loud," Ruf said. He paced in silence for a moment hoping the conversation would continue without him. No such luck. "All right, here's what happened. You know my biggest problem with the dogs is that they always come up with prob-lems, right? I was thinking about this yesterday while I was meeting with the dogs and they were coming up with *that day's* problems. Finally, I asked them why in the world they always do that. And one of them answered me. Not in front of the others, fortunately. But there it was, bigger than a mastiff riding a Clydesdale and as clear as the space between my ears, apparently."

"What on earth did this dog say?" OM asked.

Ruf shook his head, barely capable of re-counting the conversation. "It turns out that the reason they always come up with problems is, well, because…." Ruf paused. "Now, here's where the vulnerable part comes in. OM, I've got to tell you that the first thing that went through my head when I heard this was that when you found out, I wouldn't be long for this ranch."

OM smiled at Ruf. "Tell your story."

Ruf gathered his thoughts, though there was really no reason to do so. He'd been thinking about nothing other than this since yesterday. "The reason they always come up with problems is because I always *ask* if they can come up with problems. 'Do you have any problems with this?' 'Do you see any problems here?' I never realized it, but they've just been doing what I told them to do."

Ruf lay down on the porch and rested his head on his front paws. "OM, I'm really sorry about this."

OM started to speak, but Dal motioned for him to wait.

"Are you feeling vulnerable right now, Ruf?" Dal asked.

"Of course I am," Ruf said without raising his head. "I'm just waiting for OM to give me the axe."

"And when you feel like your job is threatened, what is the only thing you can care about?"

"Keeping it," Ruf said softly.

"Now, how do you usually act when you feel vulnerable? Do you ever get angry or pompous or dictatorial or irritable or threatening?"

Ruf nodded with each one.

"That's a huge realization. Now when you feel this way, you can choose to do something different. Right now, as you think about it, you are choosing not to react at all. You're just sitting with the feeling and the world isn't falling apart, is it?"

Ruf sat up and looked at OM. Obviously, the boss wasn't going to fire him on the spot. In fact, OM seemed to be looking at him with...admiration. Ruf cocked his head to one side, feeling as confused as he'd ever felt in his life.

Dal bowed to them. "Let's meet back here after lunch, and you can tell me what you think. Thank you."

He walked down the steps and out into the pasture.

It took several minutes before Ruf felt steady enough to leave he porch.

CHAPTER 8

Instant silence descended when Pek entered the hen house. *Finally*, he thought, *I'm making some real changes*. He got right to the point.

"I've received the list of under-producing hens for firing," he said in an authoritarian voice. "I'm going to review the list today and make my final decision by close of business. The hens affected by this improvement plan will have three days notice to take care of their affairs. Then, well, we don't need to speak about what will happen then. It will just happen."

* * *

Nay spent the rest of the morning tending to his duties throughout the ranch and trying to keep the peace. The pending schedule changes had irritated just about everyone so he ran around putting out fires, breaking up skirmishes, and trying to avoid an all-out civil war. He just loved it when OM brought in a new "expert."

After lunch, the managers found Dal and OM sitting under the Open Tree in the yard behind the main house. They called it the "Open Tree" because it looked like it had opened more than any other tree. The branches overhung the majority of the back yard and Nay had done some especially pleasant grazing back there.

They all sat under the tree and Dal began. "Why do we want to see how we are really feeling and what our automatic responses are?"

"Because sometimes we act angry and irritable," Pek said.

You should know all about angry and irritable, Pek, Nay thought.

"And how do we act if we are angry and irritable?" Dal asked.

Nay jutted his chin forward. "I've found the best policy is just to put it behind me and not let it bother me. That's why I don't know why we're talking about this so much. Why should I take the time and suffer the misery of uncovering all this pain when I can put it to the side and just go on with business? I can still make whatever changes are needed."

Dal dipped his head toward Nay. Nay already knew that this meant a lecture was coming.

"Nay, are you sure you can put all that 'to the side?' Are you sure it doesn't affect your performance?"

Nay felt a little irritation kicking up right now. "Darn sure about it. I've worked this ranch under some nasty conditions. If I spent all my time worrying about my feelings, I'd never get anything done."

"You're kidding, right?" Ruf asked. "You aren't trying to tell us that your emotions don't affect the way you work with everyone else, are you? I'm sure OM will back me up on this: when *your* goatee's in a wad, it's best to stay far away from you."

"So I get a little grumpy on occasion. Sue me. I'm a good manager and I do a good job. If you can't handle a little irritation, you can't handle managing on a ranch."

Nay looked to OM for agreement. OM put up his hands in mock defense and chuckled. Nay was still having a tough time adjusting to the *new* OM. "Nay, I gotta tell you that there have been entire days I've gone the long way around to the hen house just because you had your horns in a twist. *And I own this ranch*. I can only imagine how your chiefs must feel."

Nay was beginning to feel ambushed. He wanted to butt heads with someone. He turned to

Ruf. He chewed some grass to try to get the thoughts out of his mind.

"How is it that Nay doesn't have a clue how he makes people feel?" Ruf said.

Nay glared at him. *I'm gonna ram your butt if you aren't careful.*

"It's a clue none of us have until we look closely for it, and that takes courage," Dal said. "The first principle of emotions is that you *will* feel pain. If you are feeling something painful, only one of two things can happen with that feeling. You can acknowledge it and feel it yourself, or you can deny it and end up acting in ways that will make everyone else feel it.

"The only way out of pain is to feel it for yourself. Learn whatever you need to learn from it, do what it takes to respond to it in a different way, and let it go. Otherwise, you are destined to make everyone around you feel your pain."

Nay thought about this. He couldn't remember the last time someone made him think this much and he wasn't entirely sure he was happy about it. Dal definitely wasn't a consultant – he'd said as much himself – but what *was* he? "I wish I could say I don't see the logic in that," he said at last, "but I do, in a weird kind of way."

Dal smiled benignly and then turned to Ruf. "When we ended this morning, you were thinking about whether you could do something different when you felt vulnerable. If any of you find yourself sad, anxious, irritable or in pain, what way can you respond other than with the habit of anger or aggression?"

Now Nay was confused again. "But what if it's the other person who's making you irritable?"

"Then we have to ask ourselves if there is ever an excuse for intentionally being mean to someone else."

"If it's just a reaction, then it's not intentional, is it?" Nay asked, proud of his response.

"Too late for that, Nay," Dal said. "Now that you are aware that you are reacting to the pain, you can't claim ignorance. Try again."

"Well, I think if they started it, if they were mean first or if they irritated me first…"

"OK. Let's go with that. If they *started it*, as you put it, if they were mean - and we understand that we never have an excuse to be mean to anyone - then what are our options?"

No one said anything for a moment until Pek spoke up. "Got it, got it, got it. You just ignore them."

Dal tilted his head. "Is ignoring someone really any less mean than yelling?"

"Let me try," Ruf said. "If I notice that someone has irritated the fur right off of me, I can say to myself, 'hey, I'm irritated, but don't have to act like it'." Ruf stopped for a moment and added, "That doesn't sound exactly right, now that I've said it out loud."

"You're getting closer, though, Ruf. Let me add a couple of things and see what you think. In our mind, irritation may develop, but it will go away. Pleasure may develop, but it too will go away. So when we say 'I am irritated,' we would do better to say, 'I notice the feeling of irritation.' There is a big distinction. In one way, we are identifying with the emotion. In the other, we are noticing it. No matter what we are feeling, if we notice the emotion without identifying with it, we are free to choose how we respond. How does this apply to feeling irritated with a co-worker?"

Ruf responded quickly. Nay was wondering if the dog was beginning to enjoy these exchanges. "If I notice the feeling of irritation when I'm working with any of the dogs but realize that the irritation will eventually run its course, then I wouldn't be as likely to bark at them. Because when things do get better, I always feel bad about having barked in the first place. I just always thought they had to be barked at for me to get anything accomplished. I called it 'management by barking a lot.' In reality, I was barking because of how I felt, not because it was a good management style."

"That's a pretty smart point there," OM said. "What do you think you could do differently?"

"It almost seems a little funny, thinking about it this way," Ruf said.

"Perfect!" said Dal.

Nay felt like this conversation was going over his head. "Perfect?"

Dal turned to him. "I think that was the perfect answer. When you notice irritation, you can smile at how you used to identify with the feeling. It *is* kind of funny when you think about it."

"Well, once again Dal, you had me until hello," Ruf said. "This time it's the idea of smiling in front of the dogs. I've gone to great lengths to include them in all the planning and decisions, but if they see me as the kind of dog who smiles, that could be a problem."

"What about the kind of goat who smiles or the kind of rooster who smiles?" Dal asked. "We've been looking for alternatives to how we act when we notice feeling irritated, or some other negative emotion. Smiling sounds like a good alternative. Standing on two legs or chasing your tail could work too. The point is to do anything other than whatever your habit is."

"So what's the answer?" Nay asked.

"I'm not trying to get you to any specific answer. I'm trying to get you to the question. Your answer will be whatever you decide to try and eventually whatever you find that works."

Yep, this is definitely going over my head.

Dal smiled, as though he heard Nay's thoughts. Then he suggested they break for the day.

CHAPTER 9

Was confusion a key component of Wisdom Leadership? If so, Ruf felt as though he was already a seasoned leader. After each session with Dal, he felt a little more intrigued – and a lot more baffled. This latest thing about smiling was a perfect example. That made zero sense as a management tool for him.

Still….

"What was that?" said one of Ruf's assistant managers while informing him of a new problem.

"What was what?" Ruf replied.

"Your lip. It looked like it curled up there for a second."

Ruf decided to see how far he could take this. He smiled broadly and then broke into laughter. As he did, the urge to laugh became stronger and stronger. He wound up laughing so hard that tears came to his eyes.

"Ruf, I'm not sure what's going on here," the assistant said. He was clearly miffed, but Ruf kept laughing.

The other dog was quickly losing his composure. "You know, it isn't very respectful to treat an associate this way."

Ruf kept laughing.

"Especially when we're talking about such a serious matter. The new problems with the feed delivery prove that the whole goat plan won't work."

The serious expression on the other dog's face when he delivered his last complaint caused Ruf to howl with laughter. He glanced out of the corner of his eye at the assistant manager. He didn't want the dog to be *too* offended. That's when he saw the assistant manager's lip curl into a smile. Then he began to chuckle as well.

"Ruf, I'm serious about this," he said, but his own laughter caught up with him.

Soon, both dogs were rolling on the floor in laughter.

Several minutes later, their laughter subsided until the assistant manager said, "Really, Ruf, I'm serious."

Then their laughter erupted again.

* * *

The next morning, Ruf reported the laughing event to OM, Dal, Nay, and Pek. They all chuckled as he told his story and Ruf shook his head at the absurdity of the whole thing (though he had to admit it was refreshing).

As it turned out, though, Ruf wasn't the only one who had an unusual afternoon the day before.

"I was all set to do everything differently," Nay said about his experience with the goats. "But they jumped right in on me and before I knew it, I was chewing them from one side of the hill to the other. At some point, I realized what had happened, and I got even angrier. There was no way I could try that smiling thing that Ruf tried. None of this seemed funny to me. But as I thought about what to do, all I could remember was Dal mentioning chasing my tail. So I did that. Three times."

OM's eyes practically bugged out of his head. "You did? What happened?"

Nay lowered his head to the ground and shook it in wonderment. "It stopped everything on the spot. I mean everything. They shut up and when I stopped chasing my tail, I saw that their eyes were as wide as tin cans. One of the goats asked me if I had an itch. I told him it was something like that.

"The interesting thing was that it broke the tension. I wasn't irritated anymore, and we actually had a productive meeting afterward."

"Those are fascinating examples," Dal said. Ruf thought he caught a little admiration in the furry animal's eyes. "Pek, did you have any interactions with the hens yesterday?"

"Of course," Pek answered. "But we've already reached an understanding. I don't have any trouble with the hens anymore. Turns out it was just a matter of getting the right level of respect from them."

Ruf thought he saw something strange in Pek's eyes. OM might have seen it too, because his amusement over the laughing and tail-chasing stories no longer showed on his face.

"Well, I certainly haven't heard a peep from the hen house lately," OM said.

"That's right, that's right, that's right," Pek said in the jittery tone he usually didn't use when the boss was around. "And you won't, either."

Ruf turned toward Dal to gauge his reaction, but didn't pick up anything unusual. "Practicing doing something different in these situations is a good thing to continue," Dal said, as though ignoring Pek's exchange with OM completely. "We've certainly been practicing doing things the same way for a long time. You will succeed and you will fail. If you continue to practice changing your automatic responses, your successes will increase. Changing any habit is difficult and these can be particularly difficult since the way we react to people is usually something we just consider a part of ourselves rather than something that needs to be changed."

Ruf, Nay, and OM nodded. Eventually, Pek did as well.

"Now we can start to get to the real heart of the matter."

Ruf's jaw dropped. "You're kidding, right? How much more heart do we have to get to?"

"Remember when you said, 'The marrow is where the marrow is'?"

"Yeah?"

"Well, you've still been chewing on bone."

Ruf sniffed the dirt for a second before facing the llama. "Sure seemed like marrow to me." He turned slowly in a circle three times, looked up at Dal, then sat down.

Dal smiled at him and then addressed the group. "Now you are ready to begin asking yourselves the question, 'What problem am I actually facing?' Who's willing to go first?"

"I'll go first," Nay said. "What problem am I actually facing? I guess the biggest problem right now is trying to get the chiefs to accept the new schedule so I can get out of the field and concentrate on managing."

"Good," Dal said. "Now, if you didn't have that schedule problem, what would your problem be?"

"Huh?"

"If this schedule problem didn't exist or if it were already fixed, what would your problem be?"

Nay hesitated. This was about as contemplative as Ruf had ever seen him. "When we first started this discussion about change," Nay said at last, "I realized that the problem is that my managers don't put their hearts into their work."

Dal nodded. "Good. Now, if they *did* put their hearts into their work, what would the problem be?"

Nay took another moment before answering. "If they did put their hearts into their work, the problem would be that they don't take my decisions seriously enough. This schedule is just an example of that."

"What if they took your decisions seriously? What would the problem be then?"

Ruf rolled his eyes. Nay chuckled. "I coulda seen that was coming. How far does this process go?"

"As far as it needs to," Dal said serenely. "How much time and energy do you want to spend trying to fix a problem when there's really a deeper problem underneath it?"

"All right, I'll play along," Nay said, tipping his chin forward. "If my chiefs would put their hearts into their work and take my decisions seriously, I'd probably be happy. But I don't think they *would* take me seriously because they would think that I was making these decisions on a whim. So, it's not that they don't take my decisions seriously. It's that they don't realize my decisions are the product of careful consideration and that they are the best for everyone involved. I mean, OM has me running the goat teams for a reason."

"If your chiefs took you seriously and knew that your decisions were the best options, what would the problem be?" Dal asked.

Nay answered instantly. "If all that happened, I'd be happy."

"Would your chiefs be happy? Would they feel as fulfilled in their jobs as you would?"

Nay laughed and Ruf wondered if the goat was trying to use some of Dal's psychology on the teacher. "Oh, so this isn't just about *me* being happy? Why didn't you say so? I'm sure if the chiefs had their way, they would want to be included in the decision-making process from the beginning instead of just carrying out my well thought-out, perfected plans."

"Good," Dal said. "You are closer to your solution than you've ever been before."

Nay, however, did not look like he saw it that way.

Dal turned to Ruf. "Ruf, how about you?"

Ruf assumed this would be coming and he was prepared for it. "I've seen the dark alley you drove Nay down and don't particularly want to get stuck there myself. I already did your little exercise in my head."

"Great, let's hear it."

"I started with the biggest problem we have now. That's trying to redo the schedules. The first problem is that everyone is angry that the schedules are changing. The second problem is that even if they weren't angry, they would still be spending all their time finding the reasons why the schedule changes couldn't work in the first place. I already told you I figured out why that was happening."

"What if the dogs weren't angry and they stopped looking for problems? What would your problem be then?"

"Problem? What problem? I'd be as happy as a kitten in a sardine factory."

"Even kittens get tired of sardines eventually. Think further. What problem might you run into?"

Ruf found himself getting annoyed. Every time he tried to play along with Dal, he got caught in the llama's mind games. "I can't think of anything. Any hints would be appreciated."

"OK, I'll give you a hint, but I'm trying to be intentionally vague, so I can lure you down the blind alley," Dal said, smiling.

Ruf didn't smile back.

"Why did you choose certain dogs to be your assistant managers?"

"I base my promotion decisions on a dog's level of experience and his knowledge in the various areas of security, herding, and family relations."

"And you're telling me that when you have dogs with years of experience, advanced knowledge in security and herding, and the ability to interact with the family, that the absolute most you want out of them is for them to stop coming up with problems? I think you're official-ly stuck in that blind alley."

Ruf's eyes narrowed and he felt a growl coming on.

Dal continued. "Sometimes we experience things so negatively for so long that the only thing we can think of as positive is the end of the negative. Let's say you and the dogs are facing a problem. What else could the dogs do besides their regular job and shutting up? After all, you've already told us this would be your vision of perfection."

Ruf stood up, ready to bark his protest at this interrogation and Dal's attitude. But some-thing caught him up short. "Wow," he said, vig-orously shaking his head. "It took me a while, but I think I'm getting the point. My assistant manag-ers could do their usual jobs. They could shut up about all, well, *most* of the problems. *And* they could help come up with solutions. That's it, isn't it? I think that's what you were getting at."

Dal had that look of appreciation in his eyes again. "No, that's what *you* were getting at. And you got it. Good job. You're off the hook for a while."

Ruf felt a surprising sense of satisfaction.

Dal turned to Pek. "What about you, Pek. What would you say your biggest problem with hen house management is?"

Ruf's ears pricked up. For the last few meetings, Pek rarely moved, and hardly spoke except to say that everything was fine and that he understood everything now.

"I told you earlier that we had one problem and one problem only. Respect. I was not acting in a way that caused my hens to respect me. I took what you said to heart, changed my behavior, and now I have their complete and total respect. I no longer have any problems in the hen house."

OM spoke up. "Pek, I'm glad you feel you've turned the corner with the hens. But I gotta ask you something. We agreed to meet a ten percent production increase this season, but the last four days have shown progressive *decreases* each day. I know any time we try something new, things can be rough for a while, but I wonder what you think might be going on."

Pek stood motionless on the porch and seemed to be staring a hole into OM's head. Ruf wasn't sure what to make of this.

Finally, the rooster said, "OM, I just need you to give me a few more days. I need your backing on this. I *expect* your backing on this."

"Pek, you wouldn't have your position if you didn't have my backing."

Pek didn't say anything else though it was clear OM wanted more information. OM looked to Dal, who looked back at OM. They both looked at Pek. Ruf felt like he could gnaw on the tension all day and not crack through it.

When the silence continued, OM said, "Pek, I don't know what is going on. I'm just asking you to tell me what is happening in the hen house."

"Not now, not now, not now! Either you give me a few days on this or you look for another manager."

OM looked stunned by Pek's attitude and with good reason. Ruf was going to have to have long conversation with the rooster afterward.

Pek walked to the top of the steps then looked back, stabbing the deck twice before speaking. "You're just days away from the biggest production increase in the history of the hen house. Do you want to screw it up now?"

"Pek," Dal said in the voice he used to calm them down, "I hear OM trying to tell you he supports you and that he wants to know what's going on with the hens. Is there a reason you don't want to tell us what is happening?"

"Knew it, knew it, knew it! I knew this promotion was bogus from the beginning. You put us completely in charge, and then you go sticking your nose in my business. OM, what gives?"

"Pek, you clearly have strong feelings about this," the llama said. "Can you tell us what you are feeling right now?"

"Yeah, I can. I feel like you need to get off our ranch."

Dal's expression didn't change. The llama definitely had a strong constitution. "Actually, Pek, that's not a feeling. But I think I get the point. Maybe you would like to take a break."

"Break, break, break," Pek said as he rushed down the steps and stormed back toward the hen house.

Ruf watched him go, unsure what to make of any of this.

CHAPTER 10

Nay was hardly surprised that Pek was missing from the next morning's session. Nay hadn't seen the rooster at all after his tirade and he certainly didn't seek him out. It was hard to believe that they thought *Nay* had an issue with anger when Pek was capable of such a display.

The four of them sat under the Open Tree on a gleaming day. Nay hated to think it – after all, he'd known the rooster for a long time – but things were more relaxed when Pek wasn't around. Even when Pek wasn't saying anything, he brought a lot of tension with him.

Dal started the session. "Today we are going to work on understanding what the true feelings are underneath our problems. What are we feeling and experiencing that lets us know we have a problem in the first place?"

"Just when I thought it was safe, we get all squishy again," Ruf said grumpily.

"Let's start with your situation, Ruf. How do you feel when your dogs come up with problems? When they shut down your plans before you ever get to try them?"

Ruf let a little growl escape. "I'll be polite and say I get irritated."

"Try the same process we used yesterday. If you weren't feeling irritated, what would you be feeling? Is there any feeling that precedes the irritation?"

"I don't suppose anger counts."

Dal didn't respond, which Nay assumed was the same thing as saying "no."

Ruf obviously interpreted it the same way. "Well, I'm upset with them not getting the job done or always getting in the way or not wanting to change to make things work better or faster."

"You're telling me that your dogs don't get their jobs done?"

"Not that, exactly. They do eventually get it done."

"So what else could be so irritating?" Dal smiled. "I'll throw you a bone. What does it feel like when you have to come to OM to let him know that things aren't going to be done on schedule or that a new plan isn't going to work?"

"That *really* irritates me. I hate that more than anything."

OM leaned forward in his chair. "What's so bad about having to tell me something like that?"

Ruf sighed deeply. "You trust me, OM. You give me a job to do. If I don't do it, if my dogs don't get it done, then I've let you down."

"So you take it personally when things don't get done on time?" Dal asked.

"Of course I do. Are you going to tell me that isn't personal either?"

"Not yet. But I am interested in how you feel when you are standing before OM, giving him the news that something isn't going to work. Look deeper in yourself. What else are you feeling when this happens?"

Ruf cleared his throat. "This is tough."

"Yes it is. Now you know why it requires warrior courage. Why we call this the warrior path. This is what it takes to stand and face yourself openly."

Ruf's tail drooped. "It feels bad, like I've let OM down. It's kind of humiliating."

"Excellent job, Ruf. Now you understand what it means when we talk about knowing the feelings underneath the feelings. So if you didn't feel bad and humiliated, how would you feel?"

"Is there *always* an emotion under every emotion? If so, this conversation is going to take a long time."

Dal laughed gently. "No, there isn't always an emotion under every emotion. But I have a feeling there's one under this one. What would it be like for you to come to OM with news that things aren't happening on time if you didn't feel humiliated doing it."

Ruf pawed at the grass. "I still wouldn't like it. But I don't think it would be such a strong feeling. It wouldn't be such a big deal emotionally. I'd bark a lot less, probably. But now I'm wondering if you're trying to tell me I have to feel OK about things not working the right way. Am I supposed to be fine about not meeting production schedules?"

Dal waited a moment before responding. "Let's look at the work you've just done. You just went from feeling humiliated to feeling a little bad, maybe a little sad or disappointed. You said this emotion wasn't nearly as strong as your anger. In which state would you be better able to work with OM on finding a solution? If you are angry and barking or a little disappointed but otherwise calm?"

"That's one of those questions that doesn't need answering by the time it's asked, isn't it?"

"You said it, Ruf. This boils down to your realizing that you can be an effective leader, a decisive and powerful dog, even when you aren't angry. More so, actually."

Ruf cocked his head to one side. "I've never thought about my life, let alone leadership, like this before. If I'm hearing you correctly, though, the tough part of this – the warrior part – is being willing and able to tolerate feeling disappointed or sad or anxious or whatever. And remaining calm with that feeling."

Dal nodded. "The warrior leaders look within and stand openly with what is revealed. They find their true experience and their true power at the same time."

Ruf settled down in the grass, looking like he had a huge amount to think about. Nay watched him so intently that he was startled to hear his name.

"Nay, let's hear from you now," Dal said.

Nay cringed and turned his head away from Ruf. "I thought Ruf was the one on the hot seat. I'm willing to put this off until tomorrow if you think Ruf has more to learn."

"Nice try, Nay," OM said.

"Let's leave Ruf with his thoughts for now," Dal said. "You experience your chiefs as not having their hearts in their work and not taking your decisions seriously. They don't realize that you have already come up with the right course of action. How do you feel when this happens?"

"I feel riled up, of course," Nay said quickly. "And underneath that is the feeling of being more riled up."

"So what's under both layers of that emotion?"

Nay wasn't really up for this game, but he responded anyway. "I don't want to sound like Pek here, but it really feels like they don't respect my plans and decisions. They don't respect me."

"And how does that feel?"

"Not worth a darn," Nay said sharply.

"This is your warrior moment. What is it that doesn't feel worth a darn?"

Nay thought about this and felt himself getting increasingly upset. "To start, like Ruf, I don't like situations that will lead me to a confrontation with OM."

Dal shook his head. "Stay with the chiefs for a moment. What's the feeling with them?"

Nay shook his chin a few times, puffed out his cheeks, blinked his eyes, breathed out, then said, "All I can see is that it's painful. It hurts when they don't take me seriously. When they don't respect me."

"Very good. You've touched the emotion underneath the emotion. How do you think your actions would change if you became aware of your pain, but didn't let it propel you to being riled up? If you just stayed with your pain?"

"That's a lot to stay with. You mean stay with the pain right there in front of my chiefs?"

"Eventually. You might have to step away at first, but eventually your pain will be something you can experience wherever you are. Think about that. What will be different then?"

Nay tried to envision this situation. It was like trying to imagine that the laws of nature had changed. "I'm kind of a gruff character and I'm not particularly interested in becoming all peaceful and everything. I think the chiefs need a certain level of...encouragement. Sometimes this requires volume."

"Try to answer the question, Nay. How will it be different for you to experience the pain but not the anger?"

"I'm *trying* to answer the question. It's not easy. It would feel scary. I would feel vulnerable."

"If you were facing your chiefs and feeling the pain, you might feel vulnerable, but would you be at any risk? Would there be anything actually threatening you?"

Nay was feeling things that he couldn't understand. He couldn't decide whether he felt like butting heads – or lying down and moaning. "What if my chiefs knew I was feeling that way? Wouldn't I be at risk for losing even more respect from them?"

"When anyone gets angry and irritated or yells at someone else, it's precisely because they are feeling these vulnerable emotions," Dal said. "So at some level, the chiefs already know it."

"In other words, I'm busted either way."

Dal smiled. "Yes, you are. What if you didn't get angry though?"

Nay stroked his chin. "If I left it at pain, I wouldn't have to react in *any* way. I guess I'd just keep going with the meeting instead of stopping it to huff and puff like I tend to do."

"Excellent, Nay."

"Yes," OM said, "that was excellent."

Nay wasn't finished. "But I'm well known for my butting. Don't we lose our power over others if they know they can cause us pain? If someone's made me mad, that's one thing. But if they know they can hurt me, then they can take advantage of that."

Ruf sat up for the first time since Dal started grilling Nay. "That's a very good point. Once the dogs know they can get a piece of me, they'll never let up."

Dal responded. "Who is the stronger leader? The one who has to get angry to pretend he isn't experiencing any pain or the one who can withstand the pain and remain stable in the face of it? Pain is not the same thing as damage. No one likes to experience this kind of pain, but it only damages us if we let it make us angry, bitter, and hardened to the world.

"Try looking at it this way. If your dogs are doing things that make you angry, let's consider that they are shooting you with little arrows. These arrows cause a twinge of pain, but no damage. If you react with anger, then they get a response from you. They are actually in control of you because they can make you angry. If, however, you see the arrows for what they are, temporary irritations, you experience the brief pain and let it go. Then they get no benefit from shooting you in the first place. After, say, shooting you for 100 times, getting no response, and causing you no damage, they will eventually stop shooting you. They aren't getting anything out of it.

"Through this you have actually turned their arrows into instruments of healing. Your relationship with them is healing. You are teaching them that you don't have to shoot arrows at someone to interact with them. This process will serve you well on and off the ranch. And you're just getting a taste of it today."

Nay stared at Dal, wondering how he came up with all of this stuff. He had to admit, though, that he liked a lot of what was going on in his head.

"While you are still fresh with your feelings," Dal continued, "I'd like to take you through a brief exercise. Think clearly about the feelings you have discussed, whether they are pain or anxiety, shame or embarrassment. Think about the things that happen to cause these feelings and answer this question. How many other people experience situations just like these? How many other managers have ever had workers who they thought didn't respect them, or have had managers who always threw a wrench into everything?

"Now, think about how many of your workers ever feel they aren't respected or have others in their lives who seem to throw a wrench into whatever they are trying to accomplish? How many people have had these situations in their lives one way or another?

"Now realize that they all felt pain, shame, embarrassment, anxiety and other difficult emotions. Realize that they have felt your exact feelings. Think about how universal your experiences and your feelings are. You share these feelings with everyone else who lives. This pain is a connection you have with everyone who has lived, is living, or ever will live. Everyone."

Nay's head was really spinning now. So much so that he didn't even notice when Dal called an end to the session.

CHAPTER 11

Soon, soon, soon, Pek thought, scampering quickly around a table he'd set up near the back of the hen house. *Soon everything will be the way it should be*. He added some flowers to the table, thinking that was an especially nice touch.

Pek felt full of inspiration these days. Ironically, it started when OM brought that llama-guru to the ranch. It had nothing to do with Dal and his touchy-feely teachings, though. Instead, it had to do with Pek freeing his mind to seek *real* solutions to *real* problems. That's what brought him to the answer about egg production. And that's what stirred him to think of this way of facing the Dal issue head-on.

Earlier that afternoon, after skipping out on the morning meeting, Pek "extended" himself to Dal, inviting him to dinner. The only thing he instructed his emissary to say when the hen delivered the invitation was that Pek wanted to clear the air and seek common ground. He knew that would get Dal's attention.

When the *guru* arrived, he looked at the table and nodded appreciatively. In addition to the flowers, Pek had prepared the table with a large pile of oats on one side and a small pile of corn on the other. "Namasté," Dal said.

"Yes, yes, yes. Namasté." Pek realized the words came out too rapidly and told himself to calm down.

Dal tipped his head toward the table. "This looks lovely."

"No trouble, no trouble…. I wanted to make a little gesture. I figured it was time that we had a heart to heart and this seemed to be a good way to do it."

"Well, I appreciate the gesture, Pek." Dal walked to his side of the table, bowed his head toward the food, but didn't eat. "I'm curious, Pek. Why did you think we needed to have a heart to heart?"

Pek jumped up on the bench on his side of the table, stabbed a kernel of corn, and downed it quickly. "The last time we were together, I got a little hot. I just thought I should explain myself." Pek scratched at the bench, then forced himself to regain eye contact with the llama. "I've been very upset with your being here. You came here and tried to change everything and I was resistant to that. I now realize that the problem was really my outlook on all this change. Since I got so mad, I wanted to apologize to you personally."

Dal bowed his head and closed his eyes. "We all do things that we regret doing. What matters is what we do once we realize it."

Pek thought Dal's holier-than-thou attitude was going to drive him to a crowing frenzy, but he convinced himself to stay calm. "You're right, of course. I thought we could share this food." He pointed his beak toward Dal's meal. "Those are the best oats we have on the farm. I brought them here just for you, as a gesture of good will."

"Then I shall receive these oats in that spirit and thank you for your offer."

Pek felt a rush of excitement, but he had the composure to avoid letting this show. *Very soon, this llama will no longer be a problem,* he thought. He bent toward his meal and stabbed another kernel of corn, eating it more slowly this time.

Dal said a thanksgiving for the food and stuck his nose into the pile. *Enjoy your meal, guru,* Pek thought as he swallowed another kernel.

But Dal didn't eat. Instead, he pulled his nose out of the oats.

"Pek, let me ask you something," Dal said serenely.

Pek stopped eating and stiffened. "Sure."

"If someone brings me something poisoned to eat and I eat it, then I get sick. But if I know it is poison and continue to eat it every day for years until it kills me, who is to blame for my death?"

Pek felt his blood surging and needed every ounce of fortitude he had to keep his cool. "I guess you'd have to blame yourself?"

"That's right. Someone might do something poisonous to us. But every moment we go without forgiving that person, we continue to poison ourselves. Eventually this becomes far more deadly."

Pek's beak twitched. "How, how, how did you know the oats were poisoned?"

"You just confirmed it for me. Though if you look at your beak and my nose, it's not surprising that I can smell things that you can't."

Pek was speechless. His latest *inspiration* had turned into a disaster. All he wanted to do was make things the way they should be….

Dal tilted his head. Amazingly, his eyes looked sad rather than angry. "Pek, What do you want to do from here?"

"What difference does it make what I want to do? Once you tell OM, there won't be anything I *can* do."

"Actually, the problem isn't whether OM finds out about this or not. The problem is that *you* know what happened here. What are you going to do about that?"

"Are you telling me that you aren't going to say anything to OM?"

Dal looked deeply, unnervingly into Pek's eyes. "No one else has to know."

Pek felt as though Dal's gaze was hypnotizing him. He shook his head quickly. "I don't believe you."

"You can believe me. You were frustrated and felt out of control and you made a stupid move. That is the past. What is important is what you do next."

Pek felt his anger surge. "I know what you're doing here!"

"I don't know what you mean."

"You think you are so good by forgiving me. You think I owe you now."

"There's nothing to forgive and you don't owe me anything. But if I had eaten the oats, you would have done so much damage to yourself that you may never have gotten over it. And that would have truly been a tragedy."

Pek tried to hold Dal's gaze and found he couldn't. He let out a huge squawk, jumped down from the bench, and stalked away from the table. Anxiety filled his heart.

He knew the only way to calm himself was to go into the hen house and finalize the list of the hens to be sent to the slaughter the next day.

CHAPTER 12

Dal watched Pek striding toward the Open Tree for the morning meeting and allowed himself a modicum of hope. The rooster's reaction to last night's events was difficult to read. Could Pek truly embrace what Dal was trying to teach the managers? If he'd gone AWOL from another meeting, Dal wouldn't have thought so. But he'd come and that was a positive sign.

Nay and Ruf walked up together from another direction. They caught up with Pek just before they got to the Open Tree, but only offered a cursory greeting.

"Namasté," Dal said and the three returned the greeting. OM was already seated in a chair under the tree. Ruf settled down into the grass while Nay sat up. Pek stood, looking in some ways as though he was ready to bolt at a moment's notice. The rooster glared at him suspiciously and flicked a glance at OM. Dal tried to indicate with his expression that he'd kept quiet about what transpired last night, but he didn't know if he succeeded.

Dal looked away from the rooster and regarded Ruf and Nay for a moment before beginning. Then he scratched a small circle in the dirt in front of him.

"This circle represents the processes of becoming aware that change is necessary and developing a willingness to change."

He followed this with a larger quarter-circle and another little circle.

"This second circle is the processes of becoming open to our reality, developing the warrior willingness to see ourselves and our situations honestly and to see our habits, actions, and reactions that cause or contribute to our problems."

He drew another quarter of the large circle down and a third small circle at the end of this line.

"In this circle, we look at the real pain we are facing and the true cause for this pain, which we found isn't always obvious."

He drew another quarter of the large circle up and a fourth small circle.

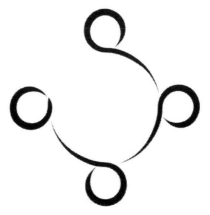

"The first part of this circle is what makes it all work. Forgiveness. The process of letting go of our judgments, our resentments, and our fantasies that anyone other than ourselves can heal us."

Pek drew tenser, as though he was ready to strike something.

Does he think I'm about to expose him in front of everyone?

Dal tipped his head toward Pek and then swept his eyes over the others to prevent anyone from thinking that he was singling out the rooster. Then he continued. "Can anyone think of why forgiveness is so important at this point?"

No one responded, which came as no surprise.

"What are we trying to do with all of this warrior work? What is this circle we are creating designed to do?"

"Create change," Ruf said languidly from his relaxed pose. "This is like the big blender we are all stuck in."

Dal's eyes brightened. "Ruf, you're always very close to the truth."

"I'll take that as a compliment," Ruf said, swatting at a fly.

"If we're stuck in this 'blender,' as Ruf puts it, then we aren't in the process of creating change are we?"

Ruf raised his head. "Okay, then it's the way to deal with change. This circle is the way we deal with being in the blender."

"That's even closer."

"You're killing me with compliments," Ruf said with a grumble.

Dal had to chuckle to himself. "Change is the reality we live in. The only time things don't change is when they are dead. So when we talk about change, we are really just talking about life. Our lives individually and the life of this ranch."

Nay leaned forward. "We learn to make wise changes with this circle. We learn the way to change in the best way for us and everyone else involved."

"*Yes*," Dal said brightly. He noticed Ruf roll his eyes good-naturedly at the goat. "Since change is always happening, it is either for our good or to our detriment. With awareness and Wisdom, the changes we make will be for our good and the good of all. Without it, change, and our responses to change, will be good for no one."

Nay stood now. "So what is the point of forgiveness in this?"

"You can't create a new future and hold on to the old past at the same time. You can't act freely and creatively in the now if your now is only an extension of your past. Forgiveness is the way we let go of the past so we can take the Wisdom from it and make now the best now that can be."

"I gotta chime in here," OM said. "This was a big one for me. I had allowed just about everyone in my life to upset me at some point and that meant I was holding a heck of a lot of resentment. What I finally realized with Dal's help is that judgment is a real deal-breaker. For instance, if I judged my managers to be irritating hotheads, then I would continue to see them that way and I would literally take away their potential to be anything different."

Nay stroked his chin. "I guess I should be glad you've seen the light, huh boss?" he said jovially.

OM smiled. "Yeah, something like that."

"Judgmental thinking comes from our erroneous conclusions about reality," Dal said. "Because our minds see us as separate from others, others become objects of our judgment. Since we believe we are legitimate judges, we mistake our judgments for reality. A quick set of questions will show this clearly, though it will probably generate an entire lifetime of thinking.

"First question: who, here, exists because he made himself exist?"

Of course, there was silence.

"Now look at all the things that had to come together for you to be who you are and where you are right now. Your parents had to have you. Your conception had to happen at exactly the right moment. If a different sperm had fertilized your mother's egg, you would be a different person. Think of all the things that influenced that timing. For us to have our bodies, brains, and minds, other people have to generate food and haul away trash. The sun has to rise and set, the rain has to fall and dry, and the seasons have to change for our food to grow.

"We are entirely made up of bits and pieces of things we eat and breathe. I am only a llama because my bits and pieces form a body having four legs, a long neck and nose, and not much of a tail. And this forms something we have decided to call a llama. The world existed before llamas existed, and it will exist long after llamas no longer exist. Even the world will come and go the same way, entirely dependent on everything else in the universe.

"This shows how completely interconnected we all are. None of us truly exists without the support of the entire universe. None of you can do your jobs on this ranch without the support of many others on this ranch. And think of everyone who supports them both at work and home. And the process goes on until we realize that we are truly dependent on and interconnected with everyone everywhere.

Dal stopped a moment to let this sink in. Ruf was up on his front legs now and Nay was paying strict attention. Pek's posture was as rigid as ever, but he didn't seem focused on Dal at all. In fact, he appeared to be looking past him.

Dal continued. "Some people call this a system, and it is, but it's really just a way of acknowledging our interdependent connectedness. From this point of view – a very old one, though it might be new to you – we see that all of us are equally required for this ranch to work. In the same way, all the parts of our bodies and minds are equally required for us to function as individuals.

"So to make a very, very long story just a bit shorter, we bring this thought to a close when we realize that we are all dependent on each other, that we are all truly interconnected, and that there is no independent existence. Given this, we cannot afford for any part of our system or of our existence to be permanently broken or dysfunctional. We cannot work to benefit one part of our system if it damages another part to do so.

"So when I judge you to be bad, to be evil, or even just to be irritating, I'm saying that is the way you are and the way you will always be. Judgment imbues permanence on states of being that are by their true nature only temporary.

"But what I've actually done is sentenced myself to living in a system with a broken piece simply because that is the way I've chosen to see things."

"Okay," Ruf said, "but if someone really *is* irritating, aren't you denying reality if you don't judge it that way?"

"That's a valuable question, but consider this: is it really true that this person is irritating, or is it only true that you experience him as irritating? If he were really, truly one hundred percent irritating, then he would even irritate himself. Everyone would react to him with the same level of irritation at every moment, always."

"Okay," Ruf grumbled, "what if they *can* be irritating?"

"That's at least a big step in the right direction. We've gone from saying someone *is* irritating to someone *can be* irritating. Even then, is he being truly irritating at his core, or do you just experience his behavior as irritating?

"Look at the difference in these two statements: 'Someone is irritating' and 'When someone does such and such, I notice the feeling of irritation.'

"The latter allows complete acknowledgment of whatever you are feeling, *but without making permanent judgments*. So, to go back to your earlier question, Ruf, we are not denying anything. What we are doing is experiencing it and talking about it in a way that doesn't make any of it permanent. We don't define ourselves by what feelings we might experience at any given moment. In doing so, we leave each new moment open to feel a different way. If you *are* irritated, then you will tend to *stay* irritated, so a past feeling has contaminated your present moment. If you notice feeling irritated and let it go, you are free in the next moment to feel peace or exhilaration."

"And that's where forgiveness comes in," Nay said enthusiastically.

Dal nodded toward the goat. "Explain that."

"If I judge that someone is irritating, then I'm going to experience him as irritating. He irritated me once and now I'm stuck being irritated every time I'm around him. Maybe even every time I think about being around him. But if I forgive him for that original irritation and I let go of the feeling, I have created the possibility that he won't be irritating and that I won't experience him as irritating in the future. So when I forgive him, I'm the one who benefits."

Dal didn't respond immediately. He let the Wisdom of Nay's words settle into the silence.

Ruf stood up now. "So you're saying forgiveness isn't for the other person?"

"Forgiveness has always been for us," Dal said. "It has never been for the other person. You can't let someone else off the hook for his actions. He has to deal with that himself. But when we forgive, when we let go of our resentment and our demand that others make up for how we are feeling, we quit poisoning ourselves with a continuous dose of despair.

"Forgiveness is what allows each moment to be new. In this free moment, we can touch the Wisdom of the problem and we are free to make new, wise choices.

Nay and Ruf looked at each other in a way that suggested that a light had been turned on in their lives. Dal hoped so. Then he looked over at Pek, but couldn't read the rooster's expression. He only wished that some of this had gotten through. Pek had many issues to deal with, but forgiveness would help with several of them.

"Tomorrow is our last meeting," Dal said. "I'll see you in the morning."

CHAPTER 13

Pek tried to take care of business the rest of the morning, but he could barely concentrate. Dal's morning session of psychobabble had been a bit of a diversion, but even then, all Pek could think about was the upcoming firings. Things had already begun to change around the hen house, but this would take efficiency up to unprecedented levels. A ten percent reduction would kick the other hens in the butts so hard that they'd be laying eggs like machines. In addition, they'd never disrespect him for another second.

Pek was about to deliver OM legendary production numbers. He'd show the boss that he deserved complete autonomy. Maybe OM would even promote him to a new level of leadership. Pek's mind swam with the possibilities.

The alarm cut through the air and shattered Pek's reverie. What was going on? OM only sounded the general alarm during emergencies. Instinctively, Pek dashed to the ranch house.

* * *

"He did what!" OM screamed. Since returning from his retreat with Dal, he'd felt a sense of peace that bordered at times on bliss. None of the normal aggravations of the ranch perturbed him the way they once did. This, however, was *not* a normal aggravation. OM sounded the general alarm and strode to the porch of the ranch house.

"Be aware of your reaction," Dal said as they stood there together.

"I am very aware of my reaction," OM said tersely.

"Don't get distracted. Just remember your Wisdom."

OM turned toward his teacher and confidant. He was already beginning to calm down. "I remember my Wisdom."

Dal's eyes gleamed at him. "I know you do. You just needed to realize that you do."

The alarm bell kept ringing until all of the key hands were gathered near the porch. Pek, Nay, and Ruf stood toward the front. OM walked down the steps and approached the rooster he'd always trusted.

"Pek, a situation has come to my attention that requires our immediate action."

Pek drew himself up. "Just let me know what you need and I'll take care of it."

"I have become aware of a plan you seem to have for increasing production and I'd like to make sure I have the details correct."

Pek's eyes narrowed and OM already knew all he needed to know.

"I've been told that you're planning a ten percent firing for today. Is this true?"

Pek stared at OM.

Remember your Wisdom. OM repeated Dal's words to himself as he choked down the desire to overreact. "I think this is a drastic measure to take for promoting egg production. Don't you think there is any way to meet our new quotas without slaughtering the low producing hens?"

"No need, no need, no need! OM, you weren't supposed to have to bother with any of this. I'm sorry you got brought into it."

"Pek, I'm not concerned because I heard about it. I'm concerned that this was your plan to begin with."

"You'd see, you'd see, you'd see. If you hadn't heard anything, the cuts would have gone through, production would have gone up, and costs would have gone down. It would have been perfect."

OM shook his head, disappointed. "I think you're missing an essential point here. I don't want anyone killed. If you are trying to scare everyone else into working harder, I can tell you from my own experience that it won't work. You just end up with hens who are so scared they can't lay effectively. I've heard this slaughter is scheduled to take place this afternoon. I want you to stop the process immediately. I think we need to work together to develop a vision and a plan for you and the hen house."

Pek drew himself taller. "OM, I hear what you are saying, but I'm just asking you to trust me on this one. You made me the hen house manager and then gave me complete leadership and a production goal. I'm going to meet that goal and you will see that I can do this job alone."

"Pek, were you there this morning? We talked about how none of us can do our jobs alone. We all require everyone else."

"This is really academic at this point, boss," Pek said, his voice eerily calm "The cuts are just going through. Even if I wanted to, I couldn't stop them now. Let's just let this play out and you'll see that I'm doing the right thing."

OM pivoted to his other managers. "Ruf! Get the dogs over to the hen house now. Stop this immediately! Nay, get the goats over there too. Send back word as soon as everything is clear."

Ruf led the charge and the dogs and goats sprinted off.

"You don't need to do this, OM," Pek said sharply. "I have things under control."

OM trusted Pek. He admired Pek. He cared for Pek. He never could have guessed that Pek was capable of such a heinous act. "No, I don't think you do."

"How did you find out about this, anyway?"

"Someone did the right thing."

"Who? I need to know who the insubordinate party is."

Before OM could even respond, a white hen stepped from behind him. "I'm the way he found out, Pek."

Pek's eyes bulged. "Lucinda? I can't believe it. After what we've been through together?"

Lucinda moved forward, confronting Pek fearlessly. "Through *together*? We haven't been through anything *together*. I've had to listen to you day and night talking about how everything was going to be perfect after you killed those poor hens. How you would finally have the respect you deserved and how the hen house would finally be silent and productive. I couldn't stand by and watch it happen, Pek. These hens give you everything they have, and they deserve better."

Pek stabbed at the ground twice and then extended his neck toward the hen. "Done, done, done! You're finished, Lucinda."

OM stepped between the two before anything else happened. "No, Pek, she's not."

Pek took a step backward. "Now I know we aren't seeing eye-to-eye on these new production goals –"

"– It's not about production. And it's not even about our not seeing eye-to-eye. It's about how you see everyone else. As their leader, you were here to serve the hens and to facilitate their growth and development. That is how the ranch benefits. *They* weren't here for *you*, Pek. *You* were here for *them*.

"You're out as the manager. You don't have any management duties over anyone as of right now."

Pek seemed flabbergasted. Was it possible that he didn't realize until just now where this conversation was going? "You're firing me?"

"I'm offering you another option. You can take the same training I did. I think if you spent three months in intense retreat with Dal at his center that you would benefit from it tremendously."

Pek crowed and flapped his wings wildly. "Three months with Dal? I'm a seasoned manager! I won't stand for it. I'm exactly the kind of firm hand this ranch needs."

The barking of the returning dogs and goats quickly drowned out Pek's tirade. OM stepped away from the rooster and looked toward Ruf and Nay.

"All clear as requested, OM," Nay reported.

"We got there in time and all the hens are safely back in their house," Ruf added. "But we have some very distraught chickens on our hands."

OM nodded slowly. "I'm sure we do." He turned back to Pek to see if he could salvage anything from this confrontation.

But the rooster was already gone.

It took more than a half hour before everyone left the ranch house and returned to their duties. OM knew he needed to let the staff take as long as they needed to process these events. Once he was alone on the porch with Dal, OM realized he needed to do a little processing himself.

"What do you think went wrong with Pek?" he asked softly.

"He couldn't forgive himself," Dal answered.

"Forgive himself? For what?"

Dal looked at OM and then looked out at the ranch. "For being himself."

CHAPTER 14

Ruf spent a great deal of the rest of the day talking with others on the ranch – including goats, chickens, and anyone else who wanted to talk – about what had gone down. Ruf considered himself a worldly dog. He'd seen war, turmoil, and tragedy. But Pek's rogue actions and the way they nearly turned the ranch on its head was one of the craziest things he'd *ever* seen.

He was still thinking about this the next morning when he sat with OM, Dal, and Nay under the Open Tree.

"Before we start," OM said, his voice a little shaky, "I want to thank Ruf and Nay again for what they did yesterday afternoon. The two of you helped to avert a real tragedy and I'll never forget that."

OM looked down at the ground and didn't say anything for nearly a minute. Ruf thought about saying something, but he was pretty sure the boss hadn't finished his thoughts. Finally, OM raised his head. "Look, there's no use going any further until we discuss Pek's actions. As you can see, he's chosen not to meet with us today."

"What's going to happen to him?" Nay asked.

OM shrugged. "What happens to him will be up to him. He declined my offers of additional training and this morning he accepted a ride from the garbage truck driver. He is already gone."

Ruf felt a strange feeling in his gut. It was similar to how he felt when he heard someone died.

"We should talk about your reactions to this," Dal said.

Nay started. "Normally, before a firing, everyone gets together and says so-and-so has to go. When they finally get canned, we are all glad they're gone. But I think there's always some fear that it could happen to us next."

"Are you worried about that, Nay?" OM asked.

"Actually, no. For some reason this seems more like it was Pek's decision. Somehow, he just didn't want to be a part of the ranch the way it should be. It's sad to see him go, though. He had more than a few quirks, but he was a good guy."

OM sat down and settled back in his chair. He looked very tired. "I'm sad he chose to leave, too."

Dal moved next to OM but faced Ruf and Nay. "Our sadness is understandable. It didn't have to turn out this way. The best we can do now is wish Pek well in whatever he chooses to do from here."

Again, no one spoke for a while. Ruf thought about the numerous after-hours sessions he had with Pek and Nay and knew that he'd miss the rooster's unique perspective on things.

Ruf looked toward OM. "Where are you going to find another manager? Are you going to open a search immediately?"

"We aren't going to need a search," OM said, his expression lightening. "I think we have someone right here who can do the job. She showed great courage yesterday. She showed the kind of compassion and dedication to the good of all that I think will make a valuable leader. In fact, I've asked her to join us today, but I wanted her to stay in the house until I had a chance to tell you about her."

OM called to Lucinda who came down and joined the others under the Open Tree.

Ruf congratulated Lucinda and then turned to OM with a chuckle. "You know, a week ago, I would have told you that the day a hen managed the hen house would be the day I started exploring my feelings under the Open Tree."

"Yeah," Lucinda said, "it's as strange as having a dog lead the dogs or a goat lead the goats."

Ruf pawed the dirt. "Yeah, exactly." He looked up at the new manager. She stood tall (at least as tall as a chicken could stand), but she didn't do so with the bravado Pek always had. "What you did, you know, took real, uh, well, it took, let's say, *plenty of feathers*."

"I'll assume that's a compliment."

"It's definitely a compliment. I look forward to working with you."

"I do too," Nay said. "But you know, we've just gone through this intensive experience with Dal. What do we do? Are you going to stay here and do this again for Lucinda?"

Dal looked at Nay and then turned and looked at Ruf. "I don't need to stay. After we finish today, you two will have been through the entire circle. And then you have OM here who spent three months studying it. You have the resources to teach Lucinda and anyone else the principles and the path we have experienced. Teaching her the circle will help keep you in it yourself."

"So what you're saying," Ruf said, "is that it's time for us to handle this on our own."

"Close again, Ruf, but not *entirely* right. You're never on your own. At least not in the usual sense of the word. Wisdom is there with you. And that leads us to the last part of the fourth circle. Receiving the Wisdom of the problem."

Dal moved to the place on the ground where he had drawn the four little circles connected by three-fourths of a large circle.

"First circle, we become aware that change is needed and we develop a commitment for that change. Second circle, we look with courage at our misperceptions of reality and identify our actions and reactions based on those misperceptions. Third circle, we look at the true pain that we are experiencing and we uncover the true source of that pain, the real problems we are facing.

"We started our fourth circle by cultivating total forgiveness for everyone involved, including ourselves. We acknowledged and let go of our judgments and assumptions. Now, and only now, are we prepared to receive the Wisdom that is inherent in the problem itself. What are we to learn from this problem and what is the solution?"

Ruf studied the circles and a question nagged at him. "If the solution is already in the problem, then why do we have to do all that work inside ourselves first?"

"That is a very good question," Dal said. He turned to OM. "Isn't it?"

OM laughed. "Yeah, I gave Dal no end of trouble on this point. I'll let him try it on you though. Maybe you won't be as hard-headed about it as I was."

Dal shook his head, laughing. "It was a tussle with you, wasn't it," he said, exchanging a fond glance with OM. "Let's use an example to make it easier. Let's review your process, Ruf. Take us through the circles so far as you've experienced them."

Ruf still didn't love being singled out, but at this point, he was willing to play along with just about anything. He moved to the top circle. "OK. When you first asked me if I thought any change needed to take place, I started thinking about my work here on the ranch. The way my assistants and I work together – or don't as the case may be – has been such a long-standing pattern that I stopped seeing it as a problem. Once I realized this, I saw that change was necessary. Things needed to function differently. Then the question was if I really desired this change, which I did and I do.

"When it came time for me to look at myself and the situation openly, I realized the way my assistants act is really a function of how I act. My normal response was to get mad and bark a lot. What I practiced changing was my response to my assistants, not getting angry every time they came to me with some reason why things wouldn't work. By itself, that caused a significant decrease in the stress. We're still having trouble trying to deal with the schedule changes Nay needs because of the goat team availability, but that's another story.

"Then came the tough part. I'm a dog, a working dog for goodness sake, and asking me to identify my pain was a little out of my comfort zone. Still, I survived it, and what I found under all my anger and constant barking was that I experienced pain when my dogs didn't do what I knew was best for the ranch. I felt humiliated when I had to come to OM and let him know we weren't going to meet the deadline. Then when we looked for the real problem underneath, I found that the real reason my assistants kept coming up with problems was that I was *asking* them to come up with problems.

"Now if we add the forgiveness we talked about from yesterday, then I've had to let go of all the irritation and resentment I have toward my assistants for being this way for so long. And I have to let go of my judgment of myself as being a bad manager to cause this problem in the first place."

Ruf looked around at the rest of the group and then shook his head quickly. "Oh, I forgot a step. When I admitted how much pain and shame I was really feeling, I had to realize that everyone else feels this pain and shame too. That didn't diminish my feelings, but it sure helped put them into perspective. Pain and suffering aren't just about me."

Man, that was a lot to say all at once. Ruf regarded his boss. "So, how'd I do coach?"

OM smiled at him and Dal said, "You're exactly where you need to be for the last step. Accessing the Wisdom."

I'm certainly ready to access something *after all of this*, Ruf thought. "Tell me what to do."

"Ruf, this has never been about me telling you what to do and we're not going to start now. When you have done the preparation, you are able to experience the Wisdom of the problem. Neither you nor your problem is separate from this Wisdom. When you now look within yourself and within the problem, you access the innate Wisdom that has been there all along. When you do it, it will be the most natural thing you've ever done.

"The deepest Wisdom is not something you get from thinking about the problem, though thinking about the problem is also useful. Wisdom comes to us between our thoughts. Ruf, I would like you to express to me your problem as you have come to know it."

Ruf let this swirl around in his head for a moment. "The problem I have been experiencing is that my assistant managers think their main function is to create or identify problems with every plan I propose."

"Good. Now, what have you learned about the cause of this problem so far?"

"I learned that the reason my assistants keep coming up with problems is because I always ask if any of them see any problems."

131

"So they were just doing what they thought you wanted them to do?"

The realization settled over Ruf like a warm blanket. "That means they have been loyal to me all along. They have been diligently doing what I asked them to do all this time."

Dal nodded. "Now is it possible to change how your assistants address the new plans and projects on this ranch?"

"Of course it is," Ruf said with absolute certainty.

"And how will you go about that change?"

"I just have to change myself. Change what I communicate to my managers. Change what I value them for."

"You were valuing them for their ability to come up with problems. What value do you see in them now?"

"Clearly, they have value because they can come up with solutions and not just problems. They can have many functions, actually, and many values."

"Look deeper into your own Wisdom now. What other value might they have?"

Ruf thought. "They have value as themselves. They have value because they have access to Wisdom too." A larger point rushed into his head. "They have value since we are all a part of the same system, because we are interconnected. Because *they* are really *we*."

Dal beamed at him. "That's exactly right."

Ruf's ears pricked up. "Exactly?"

Dal nodded. "Yes, exactly."

Ruf settled back on the grass. "Who knew, huh?"

CHAPTER 15

Nay felt proud of his friend Ruf for the break-throughs he'd made. The thought that a week ago the three managers tried to undermine OM's "latest consultant" seemed ludicrous now, given everything that happened. As Nay sat with OM, Dal, Ruf, and Lucinda, he felt a real sense of beauty in the moment – and a real sense that his life had changed for the better.

After some time, Dal said, "This is a small taste of the Wisdom available to us all. This Wisdom is from the same source as everything else that exists. So when we lead from Wisdom, we are naturally leading in a way that is based in reality. There is nothing contrived, or artificial or strained or coerced.

"But now you are at the step of action. You have sought the Wisdom of this problem, and you have received it. Now you have the choice to implement it or not. If you choose the path of virtue, you make a specific intention to make the change, and then you do it."

Dal connected the fourth smaller circle to the one on the top, completing the larger circle.

"Having chased my tail quite a few times in the past," Ruf said, "I know a little something about circles. So when I see you complete that circle, I get a feeling that what has already gone around must go around again."

"Once again, you're exactly right."

Ruf grinned and turned to Nay and Lucinda. "Don't worry, guys, I won't let it go to my head."

"Wisdom doesn't just shed light on the solution, but on the problems too," Dal added. "The more light you experience, the more the problems will become apparent. This is another reason why you have to develop the warrior courage. Otherwise you could withdraw in fear as reality becomes clearer."

"But it seems to me," Lucinda said, speaking up for her first time in her new role, "that what you originally thought of as a problem wasn't even really a problem. It was just the way for things to get better. Since things aren't perfect, what we see as problems are really windows to the Wisdom necessary for things to get better. For them to get closer to perfection."

Dal's eyes widened a bit. "That is quite an observation for your first day. And you have expressed a very important truth. This circle is beyond seeing things as problems or solutions. Problems and solutions are facets of the same experience. These experiences are our windows to Wisdom. They are our map for experiencing growth, effecting change, and finding purpose."

Dal sent a reverent smile in Lucinda's direction. "I think you're going to do just fine with this group of emerging leaders."

"Just remember," OM said, "that attaining perfection isn't our goal. Not to sound too much like our teacher here, but we always have to keep in mind that every solution comes with problems and every problem has its solution within it."

After a moment, Nay cleared his throat.

"Yes, Nay," Dal said. "We haven't forgotten you, no matter how hard you might have been hoping for us to."

"Actually I had a question first. When you initially asked us if we knew that change was necessary, it didn't take any time for us to say yes. The problems we are dealing with right now are very big. But I'm wondering how we continue to know that something needs to change or that we need to take it through this circle."

"The big obvious problems are just that – big and obvious. And each one might need to be processed through the circle many times. The ultimate change from this process takes time. We have been operating in our old patterns for quite a while, and although we might change some part of ourselves quickly, the entire system can take a while to change.

"But to your question. How do we know what needs to be changed or what the correct question is in the first place? We have three answers. We know that everything that exists in time will eventually stop existing in time. Nothing is permanent. So, we look for these three experiences. First, we look to see if we are trying to hold onto anything as if it were permanent. Are we trying to seize something that is going to disappear no matter how hard we try to keep it?

"Second, we look to see if we are angry at or are avoiding something. Have we developed an aversion to someone, some thought, or some feeling that is keeping us from seeing reality?

"And third, we look to see if we are in denial about our reality or if we just don't care about it. Ruf? Are you willing to finish your analysis with these questions?"

"At this point, I think I could handle any question you come up with."

"Good. Can you see anywhere you were trying to hold onto something that wasn't actually hold-able in the first place?"

"Yes. I was really seeking approval from OM. And anytime I felt I didn't have it, I was upset and miserable. There are going to be times OM is pleased with how things are going and there are going to be times when he isn't. If I keep letting that bother me like it has, then I'll never be free to try new things on the ranch. I'll be too worried about how OM feels about me.

Dal dipped his head to speak again, but Ruf preempted him. "And I think I already know the answer to the other two. I developed quite a bit of anger toward my managers because of their behavior. I was yelling and barking all the time. And as for not caring, that's where I was when you came onto this ranch. I just didn't care about improving things anymore. So, there. I had all three of those experiences."

"Great examples, Ruf," Dal said. "When we have an obvious problem, we have something to put in the circle. And when we find any of these three in our lives in any way, then this is another indication that we have something to put into the circle. Does that answer your question, Nay?"

"I think it does."

"Good. Now we can look at your situation."

Dal walked Nay through the same process he took Ruf through. Nay looked at his problem with his team leaders not respecting him the way he thought they should. He found that by expressing respect and adhering to his own integrity, what he was really seeking in his leaders, he would have. He knew that the change had to start with him and he was certain he could handle it.

The morning discussion went on much longer than usual. Nay wasn't eager for it to end and he could tell that the others felt the same way. At last, though, Dal bowed his head for a moment of silent contemplation and then addressed the gathering.

"My friends, I want you all to know that I have benefited from being with you, and I am very grateful for the work you have done starting your own journeys. You will eventually realize that you have always been on this journey. But now you have the path of Wisdom to be your guide. In a short time you have developed courage and honesty. You will lead this ranch into much greater harmony within and with all."

Then Dal said, "Namasté." and he turned and walked slowly to the driveway at the side of the house, where his trailer was waiting for him.

EPILOGUE

That afternoon, Ruf met with the dogs. All dogs were present, including the assistant managers, working dogs, and security. Nay had goat team leaders filling in for ranch security so Ruf could address his entire staff.

The dogs crowded together in a circle. Ruf made his way through to the center. Once there, he took a moment to breathe, then looked around at those assembled. He realized he was seeing his dogs in a way that he never had before. This pack of dogs that had caused him so much grief and agony was the most loyal group of workers and managers that anyone could want. All they lacked was a leader who was enough of a warrior to seek Wisdom.

And now they had one.

"Thank you all for coming today," Ruf began, and then realized this was a stupid way to start since this was a mandatory meeting. "What I mean is that I am glad to see you all here today. I'm glad that we work together here on this beautiful ranch."

He looked out again into the sea of faces staring at him. He saw effort, determination, and skill there. "We have faced many challenges together and we will no doubt face many more. But I want to express to you here today that I wouldn't want to face the big challenges, or the little ones of our day-to-day routine, with anyone else. I have an announcement that I think will please everyone here. After much discussion, the goats have decided not to implement their new team schedules. We can cancel all the drastic changes that we had to plan and go back to the previous schedules that have worked so well for us."

Commotion followed immediately. Paws shot up in the air. Murmurs spread throughout the pack. Ruf pointed to one of his assistants. "Kip? What are your thoughts?"

Kip stepped forward. "Boss, that's not going to work." Shouts of agreement accompanied this. "Food shipping schedules have already been changed, vendors notified, and the memos have already gone out ranch-wide."

The pack erupted. Dogs were barking, pointing here and there, and Ruf even heard growling. This meeting was no different from any of the others.

Except in one extremely important way. Ruf took a moment before he said anything. He thought about the Wisdom he had gained about himself, his dogs, and his place on the ranch. Then he stood on his hind legs in the middle of the quarrelling pack of working dogs – just stood there until the attention turned back to him.

Eventually, the dogs fell silent.

"In the future," Ruf said authoritatively but not angrily, "we dogs will be included in the process of making changes in the ranch. Especially changes that affect us directly like these goat schedules did. Today, however, we have a situation that we didn't create, but that we must address nonetheless. The new goat schedules were created for reasons that, let's say, were less than well thought out. So, after Nay and the goats did some thinking, they cancelled the new schedules. First, we had to change one way and now we have to change back after much hard work. I applaud that hard work, which is what you always deliver to me. My friends and my co-workers, I have a different question for you, and I look forward to your answers.

"Given that we must change our schedules back does anyone have any suggestions as to how we can accomplish this?"

The pack didn't respond much in any way at first. *They don't know what to do*, Ruf thought. But after a minute, a paw went up in the group. Ruf waited and another dog raised his paw. Several more followed.

Ruf turned a complete circle to see everyone in the pack. By the time he finished his circle, every dog in the pack had a raised paw.

For the second time that day – and the second time ever – Ruf saw his dogs in a way he never had before. He sat in the middle of all of the dogs with their paws in the air. He turned toward Kip and pointed.

Kip spoke up. "Yeah, Boss. I think the biggest problem is going to be with feed delivery since they require a thirty-day notice of any changes. We just notified them of an emergency change because of the new schedules, which they accommodated, but they might not do that twice in one week. If not, we are looking at thirty days where feeding schedules might be off before things get back to normal. But I think we could come up with a plan to cover us for those thirty days."

Many heads nodded throughout the gathering of dogs.

Ruf felt his spirit soar. The best changes were about to begin.

Made in the USA
Middletown, DE
31 March 2021